# BUILD IT SIMPLE

## Practical Projects and Inventive Solutions
## for Home and Garden

W0114517

Storey Publishing

The mission of Storey Publishing is to serve our customers by publishing practical information that encourages personal independence in harmony with the environment.

Edited by Hannah Fries, Sarah Guare Slattery, and Rob Wotzak
Art direction by Bredna Lago
Book design by John Clifford
Text production by Jennifer Jepson Smith

Illustrations by © Steve Sanford
Diagrams by Ken Braren, edited by Steve Sanford, 9, 11 t.l., 65 t., 71, 81, 85 b., 86 m., 89 t.

Text © 1977, 2025 by Storey Publishing
Previously published as *HomeMade* (Storey Publishing, 1977).

Take proper safety precautions before using potentially dangerous tools and equipment or undertaking potentially dangerous activities. Be alert and vigilant while operating heavy machinery.

All rights reserved. Hachette Book Group supports the right to free expression and the value of copyright. The purpose of copyright is to encourage writers and artists to produce the creative works that enrich our culture. The scanning, uploading, and distribution of this book without permission is a theft of the author's intellectual property. If you would like permission to use material from the book (other than for review purposes), please contact permissions@hbgusa.com. Thank you for your support of the author's rights.

The information in this book is true and complete to the best of our knowledge. All recommendations are made without guarantee on the part of the author or Storey Publishing. The author and publisher disclaim any liability in connection with the use of this information.

The publisher is not responsible for websites (or their content) that are not owned by the publisher.

Storey books may be purchased in bulk for business, educational, or promotional use. Special editions or book excerpts can also be created to specification. For details, please contact your local bookseller or the Hachette Book Group Special Markets Department at special.markets@hbgusa.com.

**Storey Publishing**
210 MASS MoCA Way
North Adams, MA 01247
storey.com

Storey Publishing is an imprint of Workman Publishing, a division of Hachette Book Group, Inc., 1290 Avenue of the Americas, New York, NY 10104. The Storey Publishing name and logo are registered trademarks of Hachette Book Group, Inc.

ISBNs: 978-1-63586-824-1 (paperback); 978-1-63586-825-8 (ebook)

Printed in China by Toppan Leefung Printing Ltd. on paper from responsible sources
10 9 8 7 6 5 4 3 2 1

TLF

Library of Congress Cataloging-in-Publication Data on file

# CONTENTS

# I Can Make That!

This book is about saving and savoring. It was written to help you save money, resources, and that most precious of all your possessions: time. You'll find suggestions that will likely make work on your future projects a little easier. And we hope these projects help you savor the joys of keeping a home or tending a garden—whether it's the satisfaction of having wood piled neatly by the door or the particular thrill of growing early spring greens in a cold frame.

It is our hope that as you look through this book, you stop several times and say, "That's for me. I need it." And then, of course, you build it and find it works just as you hoped it would.

We hope that you don't say, "I'd like that, but I never could build it." Have faith in your own abilities and test them as well. Most of these projects are simple to build. You don't need the skills and experience of a carpenter, nor the array of power tools. Common sense is helpful and should steer you as you fit some of these ideas to your own individual needs. As for equipment, basic hand tools are all that are needed.

Have fun. Trust yourself. Savor the adventure.

# For the
# Home

# SAWHORSE

Sawhorses are a workshop must-have with many uses, from sawing to painting and scaffolding. These elevated workstations will save strain on your neck and back.

There's nothing fancy about this sawhorse, but it has several good points. And one of them is that the legs are braced in two directions. That makes it a steady sawhorse, guaranteed not to wiggle and twist when you're sawing on it.

If you build a pair, you may want to adjust the size to match your height or the size of your projects, but as drawn it should work well for most people and tasks. For a sturdier model, make the legs using 2×4s and inset them 1 inch into the 2×6 top. Two of these can be handy, as legs for a temporary workbench or to hold lengthy lumber for sawing.

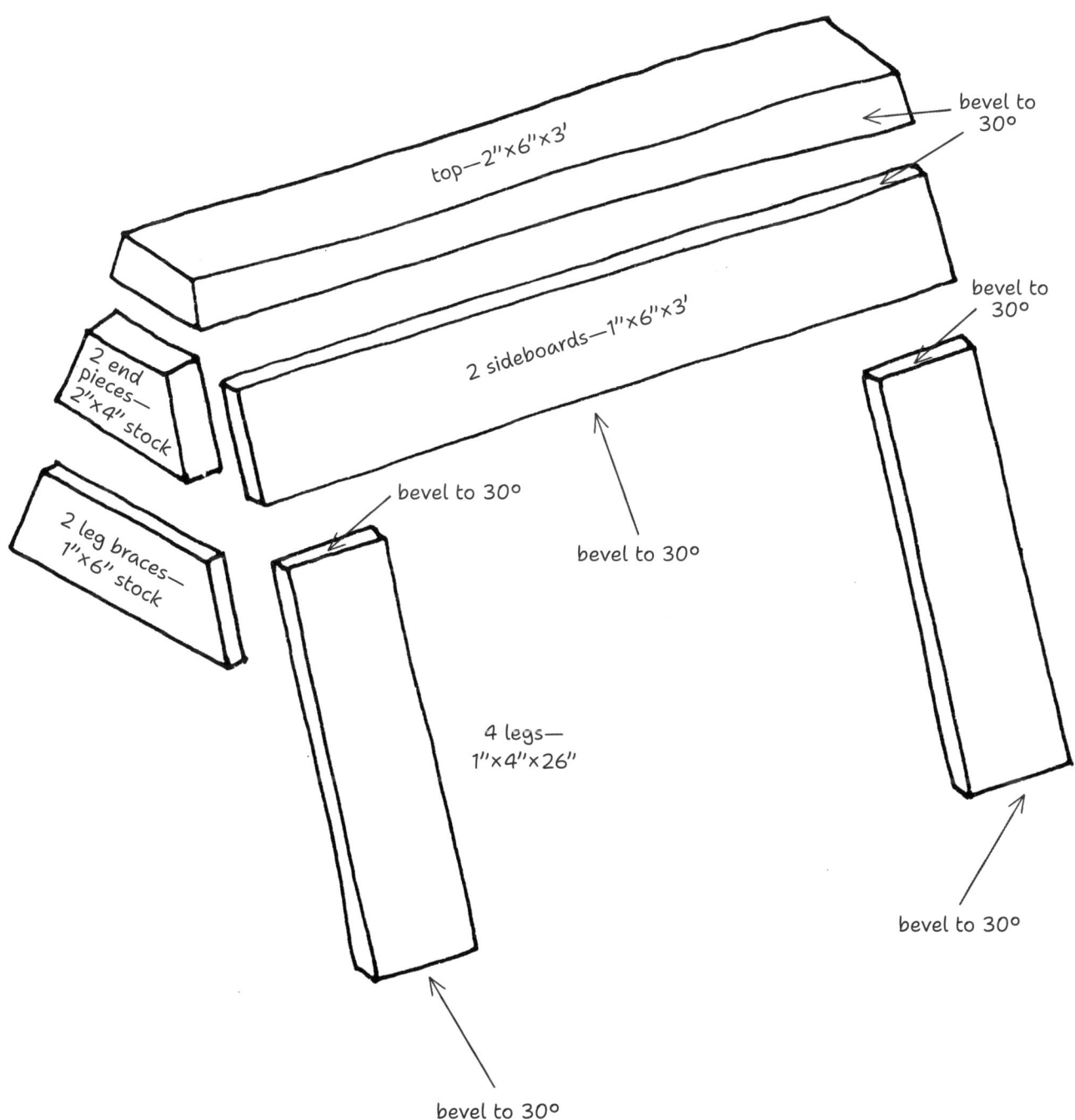

top—2"×6"×3'

bevel to 30°

bevel to 30°

2 end pieces— 2"×4" stock

2 sideboards—1"×6"×3'

bevel to 30°

2 leg braces— 1"×6" stock

bevel to 30°

bevel to 30°

4 legs— 1"×4"×26"

bevel to 30°

bevel to 30°

# CARPENTER'S TOOLBOX

If you've got several scraps of plywood or wide boards lying around, you have nearly everything you need to build a small toolbox. Add an old broom handle and some fasteners and you're good to go.

Load it up in your workshop with the tools you need for that job at the other end of the house or somewhere outside, and chances are you will save yourself a trip or two back to the shop. This strong toolbox is a good size—big enough for a framing square, a 2-foot level, or several woodworking clamps.

The dowel can be fixed into place by drilling holes through the end pieces, then gluing the dowel in position. And if you're the kind who loses tiny tools such as drill bits, make a compartment or two at one end of this toolbox using a few small boards. If the partitions for the compartments are no more than 3 inches high, they will not interfere with the placement of larger tools.

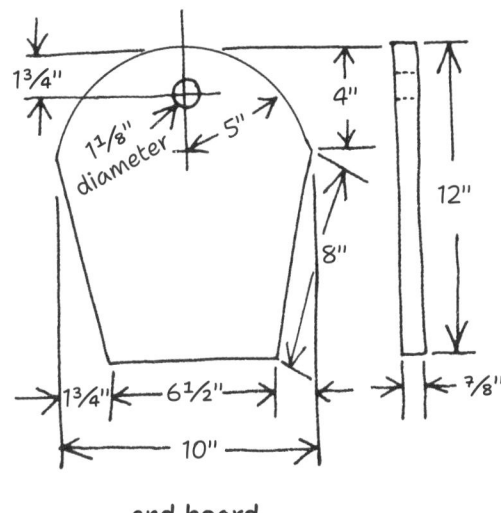

**end board**

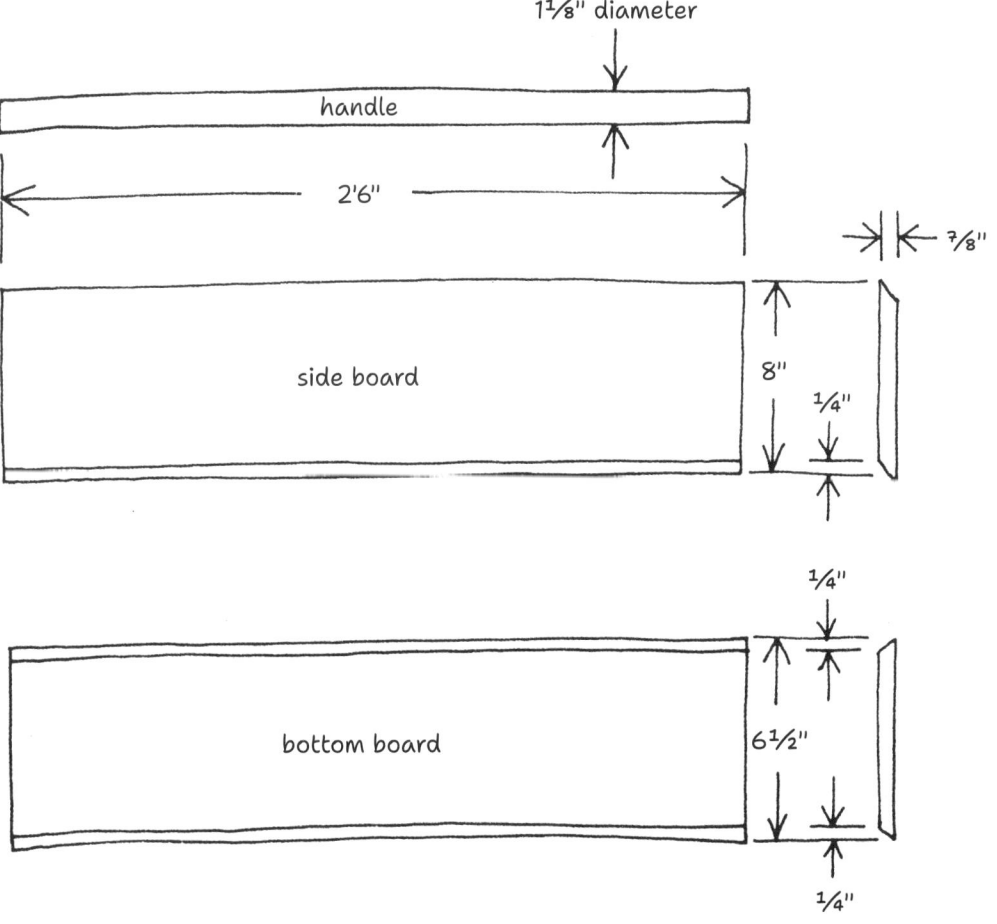

# WORKBENCH

A workbench is a must. It should be big enough to handle a variety of jobs, sturdy enough that you never worry about its strength, and not so fancy that you hesitate to use it for fear you may mar it.

This one fills all of those requirements. It is 6 feet long and 28½ inches wide, which is a good working size. If you use heavy-duty construction screws instead of nails to fasten everything together, it will be sturdy.

All of the lumber required for this is easily obtained, being either 2×4 or 2×10. Three pieces of 2×10, each 6 feet long, are needed to support the top. Alternatively, you can use a sheet of ¾-inch plywood for a flatter work surface. The ¼-inch MDF top and shelf can be cut from one 4 × 8-foot panel. You'll need three 10-foot 2×4s and two 8-foot 2×4s for the legs and bracing.

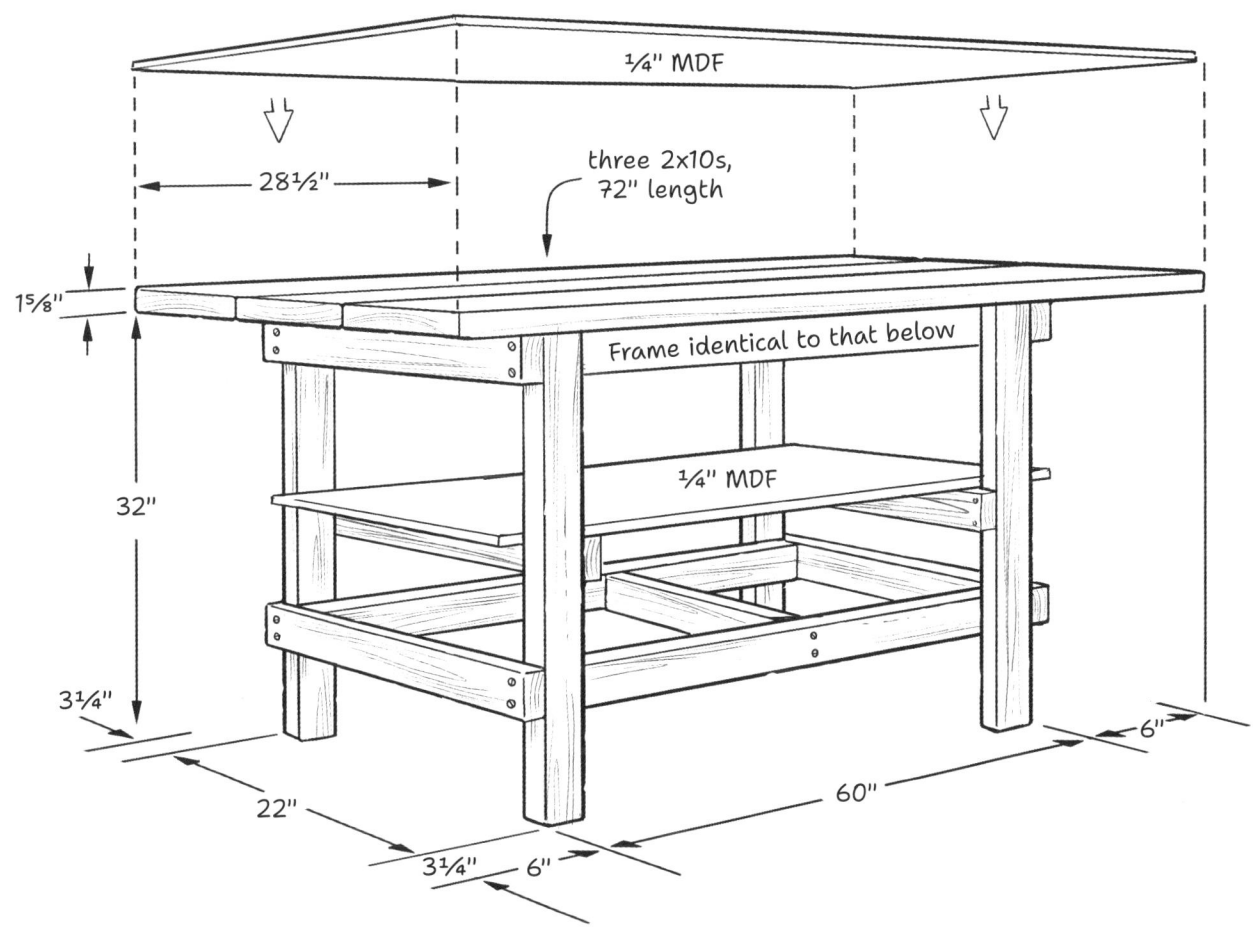

¼" MDF

28½"

three 2x10s,
72" length

1⅝"

Frame identical to that below

¼" MDF

32"

3¼"

22"

3¼"    6"

60"

6"

This exploded view shows the
¼-inch MDF top and shelf,
which will take a lot of abuse.

# BASEMENT CLOSET

That space under the basement stairs is usually wasted, or it is a catchall for unwanted or unmended articles. A compact closet could make better use of this space, or at least help to hide the clutter.

Start by hanging a plumb bob from the very top ends of each stair stringer, and marking the spots on the basement floor that are directly under those ends—these will be the front corners of the closet. Cut and lay pressure-treated 2×4s on the floor as the base of the closet—a strip of poly sheeting or sill seal between the wood and the slab is a good idea for moisture protection. Secure the 2×4s with expansion bolts or concrete screws. Next cut 2×4 studs to fit between the base you just created and the stair stringers above, beveling and notching the top ends so they fit snugly around the stringer.

Choose where you want to install shelves and fasten horizontal 2×4s as blocking between the studs on each side of the closet to support the shelves. If you plan to install a door, frame out the door opening before closing in the walls. Add a battery-operated motion-sensor light to make it easy to find things in the closet.

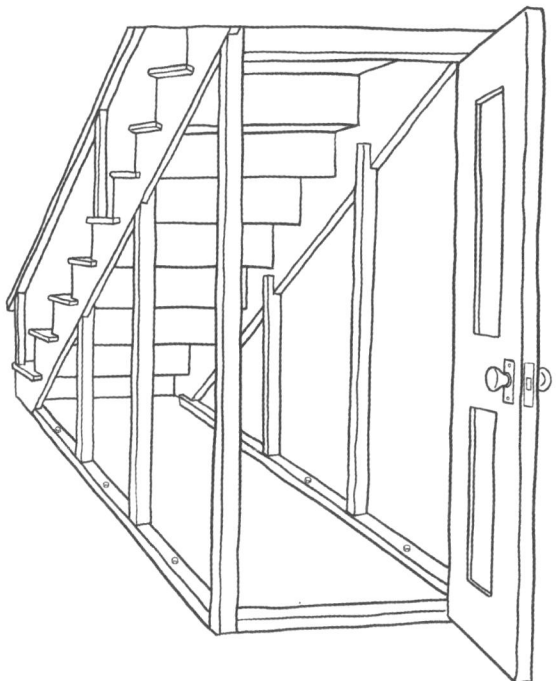

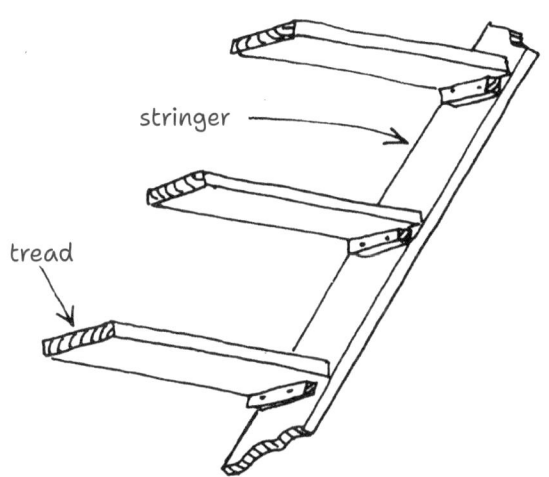

Space the studs to fall on the seams of the wall panels you plan to use.

The stringers are the long, structural boards that support the steps or treads.

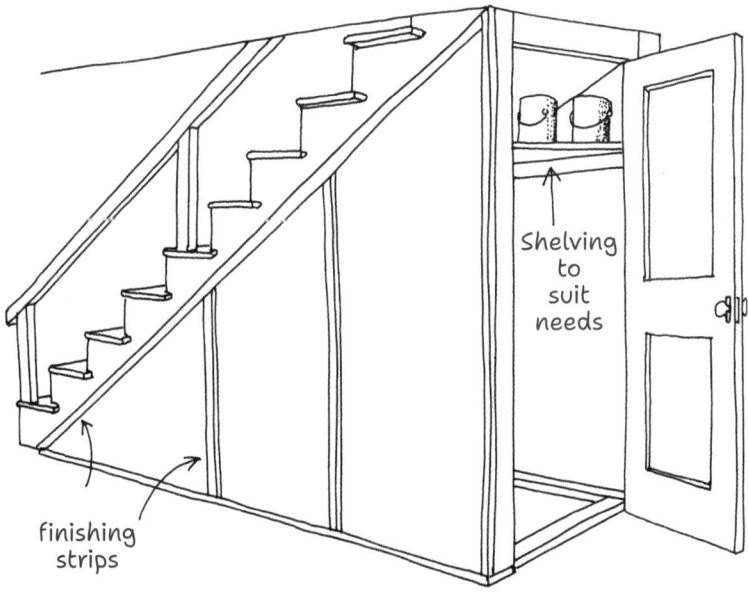

Shelving to suit needs

finishing strips

The closet walls could be made from plywood, composite wall panels, water-resistant drywall, or other sheet goods suitable for basement walls.

# POTTING BENCH

Whether you're repotting that old begonia or shifting a hundred tomato plants from flats to peat pots, a potting bench is invaluable and makes the job a pleasure. Don't have it double for any other purpose or it will be a cluttered nuisance.

Here are two models. One is freestanding. The other can be built to be fastened to the wall studs in your garage or another outbuilding. Build either to the height you prefer (32 to 36 inches is usually about right) and make it roomy in depth, yet not so wide that it is difficult to reach across. Four feet is a convenient length. Make it rugged—2×4 framing lumber is best. On the freestanding model, a shelf underneath will provide storage space (great for those extra clay pots) and brace the bench as well.

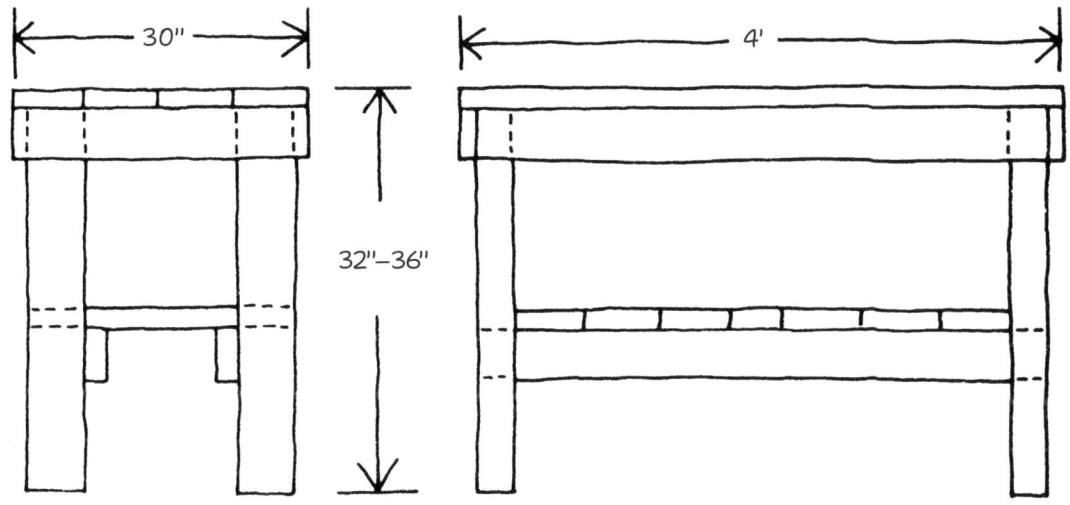

For this freestanding potting bench, you'll need three 10-foot 2×4s, one 12-foot 2×4, one 14-foot 2×4, and two 8-foot 2×8s.

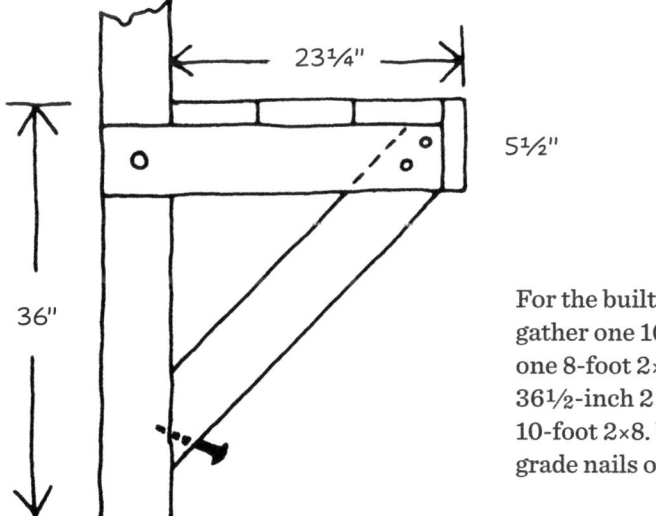

For the built-in bench, gather one 10-foot 2×4, one 8-foot 2×4, one 36½-inch 2×6, and one 10-foot 2×8. Use exterior-grade nails or screws.

# BOOTJACK

Use this bootjack whenever you come in from inclement weather, to save long hours of miserable sweeping and mopping.

Let's say it's fall and you're already thinking of winter, of storing food and wood in the woodshed, of mud and snow tracked into the house—all day every day. Do something about it. Make this bootjack. Install it right outside the back door, handy for use. And make a place near the back door (inside of course) where the boots can be dropped to dry and be used again. This bootjack (¾″ × 6″ × 24″) can be made in a few minutes by cutting a "V" notch in one end of a short board and fastening a small block of wood underneath to get the notch up off the ground.

# SAWBUCK

If you want a dull chainsaw and a sore back, cut up logs while they're lying on the ground. This sawbuck can be made in only a few minutes and will save you hours of effort and headache.

Use sturdy materials like two 8-foot 2×8s and carriage bolts with nuts and washers, and link the two ends with two crosspieces. It will last a lifetime of hard work if bolted together securely.

Make it a little taller than you think it should be, and then cut it shorter after you try it out if the height isn't quite right for you.

# FUEL SLED

If you're moving small logs before cutting them, a sled of some kind is a must. And sleds are nearly as useful over mud or dry ground as they are over snow.

The runners on this sled are old skis (cheap at any tag sale or thrift store), cut down to 4 feet in length. A 3-foot block of sturdy hardwood, at least 2×8, is fastened to each ski to raise the load 8-plus inches above the snow or ground. Bolt two pieces of 4×4 oak, about 3 feet in length, to the raised runners as crosspieces to carry the load. Fasten a heavy ring bolt through the center of the front cross member and use a short length of light chain—or, with small loads, a length of 1-inch rope—to secure the load.

Purchasing the wood for this could be expensive; you should use what you have or can find. Just make sure it's durable and strong.

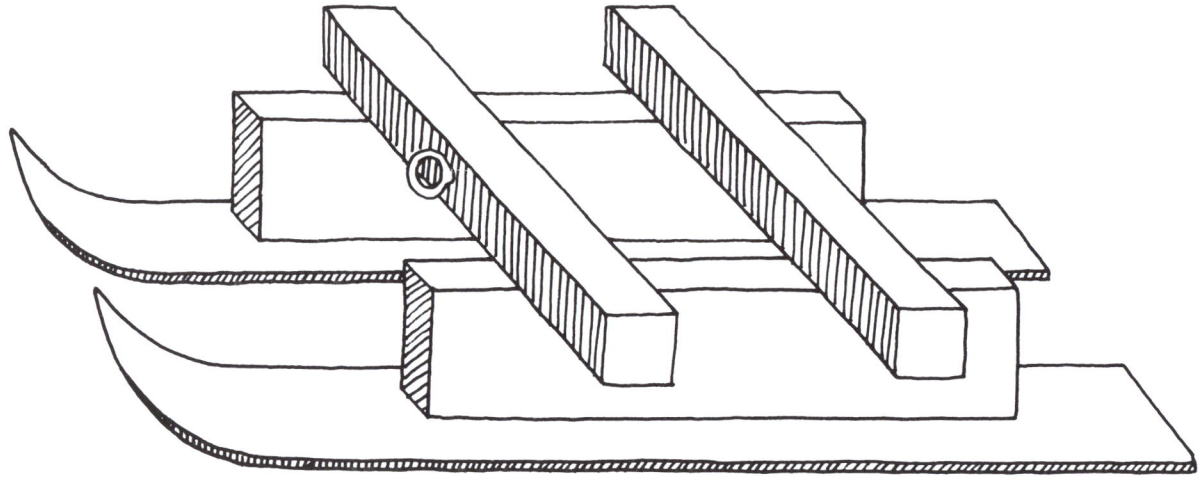

# STOVEWOOD HOLDER

Place this holder near your woodstove and save yourself from making multiple trips to the woodpile outdoors. It's handier than an old-fashioned woodbox, and neater, too.

A rack like this, built of 1½-inch (or larger) pipe, can either be welded or made from threaded pipe fixtures. Black plumbing pipe is fine, but add a coat of paint or just use galvanized pipe to avoid rust and keep it looking good for years.

This rack is about 4 feet tall, 5 feet long, and 18 inches wide, with 6-inch legs so the chips and sawdust that fall from the logs can be swept up from underneath. Make yours to fit in your space for wood storage.

Carpenter's Toolbox,
page 6

# WOODBOX

In a home where wood is being burned, this woodbox, with one door that opens inside the house and another that opens outside, is a must.

It will save miles of carrying each winter for the woodbox filler, it will prevent the loss of heat caused by going in and out during wood-carrying trips, and there will be no tracking in of sawdust, snow, and other debris.

The inside door opening is about 4 square feet and up off the floor for easier unloading. Add doorstops and weather stripping to keep out drafts and unwanted critters. The woodbox on the outside must be sturdy to take the hammering of loads of stovewood. The top should be sloped to let rainwater drain off, and the box itself shouldn't be where snow will slide onto it from the roof. It's also a good idea to insulate with rigid foam in cold climates. Insulating the doors inside will do much to keep out the cold. As an alternative, the roof can be hinged.

Even if it doesn't have a door to the indoors, building a small shed like this near your house will still keep you from digging for logs in the snow—if you remember to periodically refill it from your main woodpile.

inside view

outside view

# OUTDOOR STORAGE BINS

If your time, ambition, or money stops short of a root cellar, there are other possibilities.

Large containers, such as heavy-duty plastic bins or galvanized steel garbage cans, can be buried in the ground or covered with leaves or hay to serve as good root vegetable containers. Brand-new containers are a fine choice, but you may be able to source used containers for little to no money from local businesses that use or produce bulk food products. Whatever containers you choose, there are a few simple rules for their use.

**Ground Rules**

1. Place them so moisture drains away from them. A puddle near them will drain into the container and freeze the crops, or it will settle around the container and freeze it shut.
2. Use tops on all of them to discourage rodents.
3. Choose a metal container for the most reliable resistance to pests.
4. Cover heavily with hay or leaves so the stored goods may be retrieved no matter the weather.

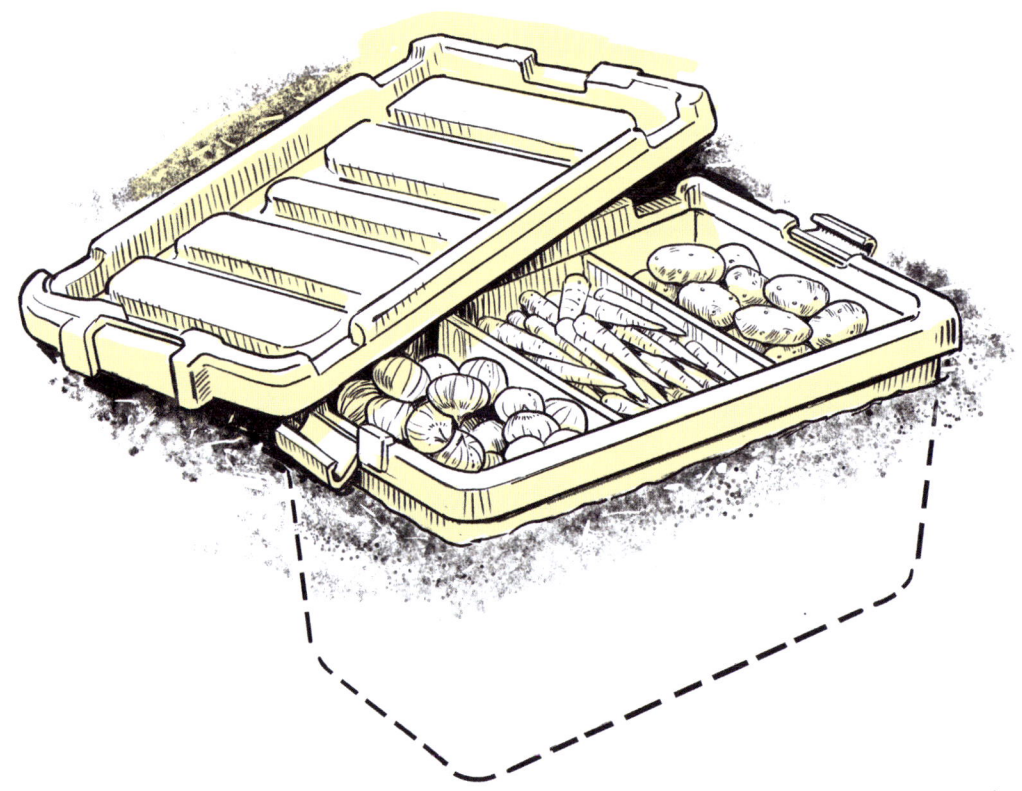

# Garbage Can Storage

A garbage can sunk in the ground makes a fine mini root cellar.

# Barrel Pit Storage

A barrel buried in the ground makes an inexpensive and effective storage container. After each layer of vegetables, pack a layer of straw and then cover and bury the barrel.

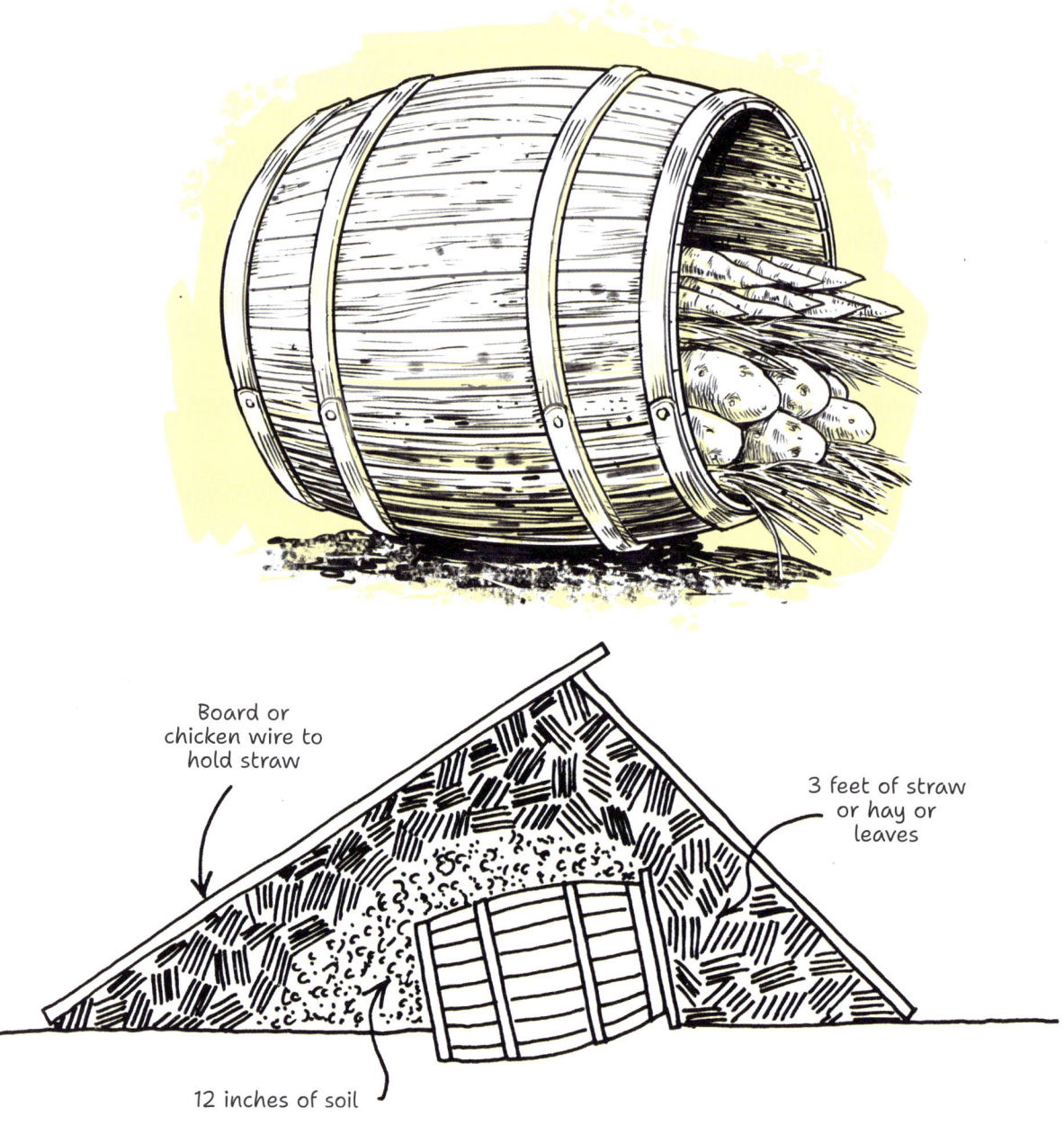

Board or chicken wire to hold straw

3 feet of straw or hay or leaves

12 inches of soil

# Rodent-Resistant Box

If you want a larger or custom-size root cellar, go one step further and construct a rodent-resistant box. It's built with a light wooden frame, lined with rigid foam insulation, and it has an exterior protective coating of hardware cloth. The top should fit tightly to the box, and, when filled, the box should be covered with a deep layer of hay or some other insulating material. This will make it easy to get into during the winter, even when snow has covered the layer of hay.

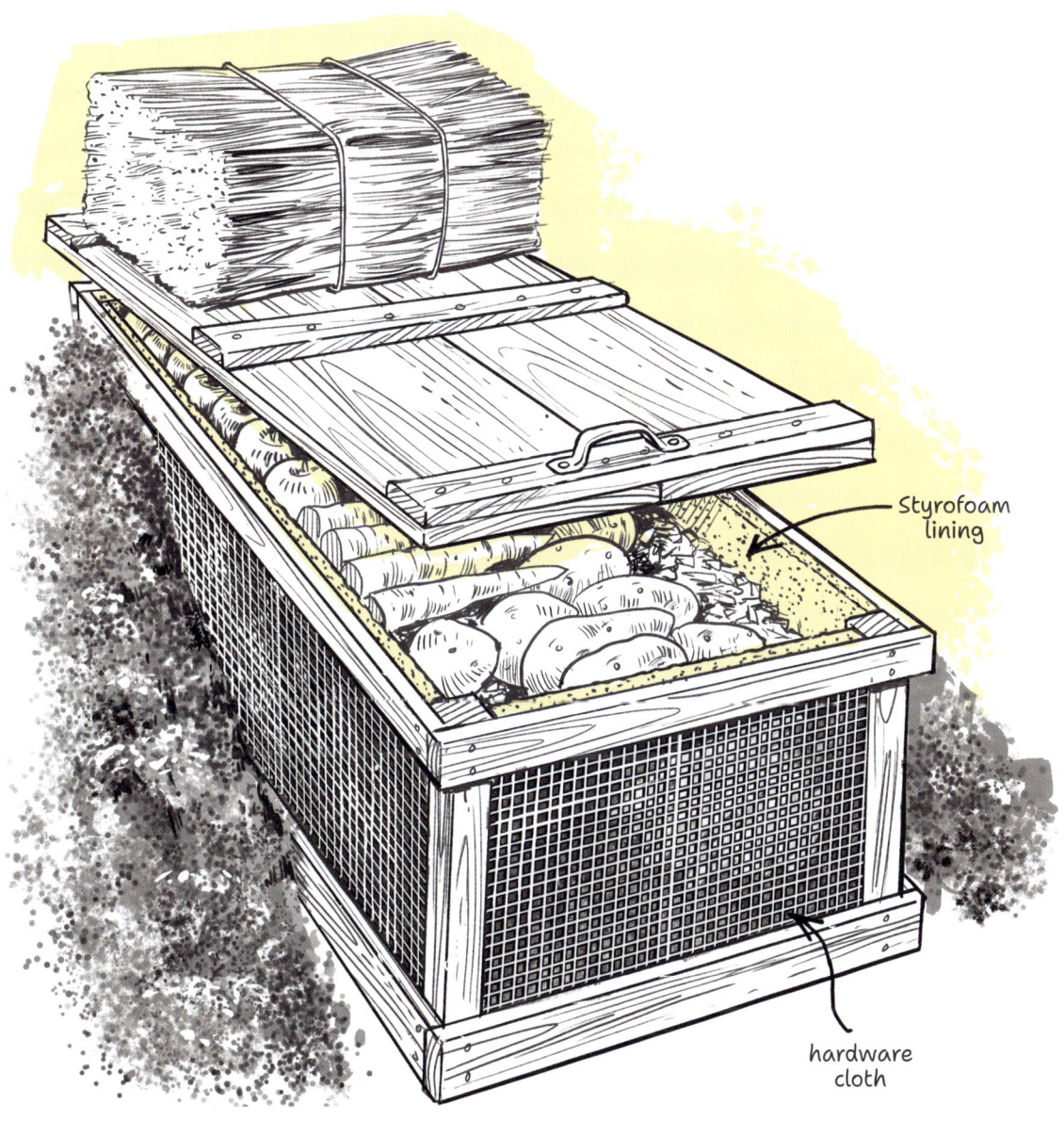

Styrofoam lining

hardware cloth

## Ideal Vegetable Storage Conditions

Each vegetable has its "ideal" conditions for storage, and of course a compromise is necessary when storing more than one variety. The following table lists ideal storage conditions and storage life expectancies.

| Vegetable | Temperature (°F/°C) | Relative Humidity (%) | Approximate Storage Period |
|---|---|---|---|
| Asparagus | 32–35/0–2 | 95–100 | 2–3 weeks |
| Beans, green or snap | 40–45/4–7 | 95 | 7–10 days |
| Beans, lima | 37–41/3–5 | 95 | 5–7 days |
| Beets, bunched | 32/0 | 98–100 | 10–14 days |
| Beets, topped | 32/0 | 98–100 | 4–6 months |
| Broccoli | 32/0 | 95–100 | 10–14 days |
| Brussels sprouts | 32/0 | 95–100 | 3–5 weeks |
| Cabbage, early | 32/0 | 98–100 | 3–6 weeks |
| Cabbage, late | 32/0 | 98–100 | 5–6 months |
| Cabbage, Chinese | 32/0 | 95–100 | 2–3 months |
| Carrots, bunched | 32/0 | 95–100 | 2 weeks |
| Carrots, mature | 32/0 | 98–100 | 7–9 months |
| Carrots, immature | 32/0 | 98–100 | 4–6 weeks |
| Cauliflower | 32/0 | 95–98 | 3–4 weeks |
| Celeriac | 32/0 | 97–99 | 6–8 months |
| Celery | 32/0 | 98–100 | 2–3 months |
| Collards | 32/0 | 95–100 | 10–14 days |
| Corn, sweet | 32/0 | 95–98 | 5–8 days |
| Cucumbers | 50–55/10–13 | 95 | 10–14 days |
| Eggplants | 46–54/8–12 | 90–95 | 1 week |
| Endive or escarole | 32/0 | 95–100 | 2–3 weeks |
| Garlic | 32/0 | 65–70 | 6–7 months |
| Horseradish | 30–32/-1–0 | 98–100 | 10–12 months |
| Kohlrabi | 32/0 | 98–100 | 2–3 months |
| Leeks | 32/0 | 95–100 | 2–3 months |
| Lettuce (head) | 32/0 | 98–100 | 2–3 weeks |

| Vegetable | Temperature (°F/°C) | Relative Humidity (%) | Approximate Storage Period |
|---|---|---|---|
| Melons, cantaloupe or muskmelon | 32–45/0–7 | 85–90 | 2 weeks |
| Melons, honeydew | 45/7 | 90–95 | 3 weeks |
| Melons, watermelon | 50–60/10–16 | 90 | 2–3 weeks |
| Mushrooms | 32/0 | 95 | 3–4 days |
| Onion sets | 32/0 | 65–70 | 6–8 months |
| Onions, dry | 32/0 | 65–70 | 1–8 months |
| Parsnips | 32/0 | 98–100 | 4–6 months |
| Peas, green | 32/0 | 95–98 | 1–2 weeks |
| Peppers, sweet | 45–55/7–13 | 90–95 | 2–3 weeks |
| Potatoes, early crop | 40/4 | 90–95 | 4–5 months |
| Potatoes, late crop | 38–40/3–4 | 90–95 | 5–10 months |
| Pumpkins | 50–55/10–13 | 50–70 | 2–3 months |
| Radish, spring | 32/0 | 95–100 | 3–4 weeks |
| Radish, winter | 32/0 | 95–100 | 2–4 months |
| Rhubarb | 32/0 | 95–100 | 2–4 weeks |
| Rutabaga or turnip | 32/0 | 98–100 | 4–6 months |
| Salsify | 32/0 | 95–98 | 2–4 months |
| Spinach | 32/0 | 95–100 | 10–14 days |
| Squash, summer | 41–50/5–10 | 95 | 1–2 weeks |
| Squash, winter | 50/10 | 50–70 | 1–6 months |
| Sweet potatoes | 55–60/13–16 | 85–90 | 4–7 months |
| Swiss chard | 32/0 | 95–100 | 10–14 days |
| Tomatoes, ripe | 55–70/13–21 | 90–95 | 4–7 days |
| Tomatoes, mature green | 55–70/13–21 | 90–95 | 1–3 weeks |

# INDOOR STORAGE BINS

Ever need just a handful of soil in the winter but your garden is down there under 2 feet of snow? You know the helpless feeling.

Avoid it by storing soil—as well as sand, compost, and any other materials you may need—in bins or cans near your potting bench in your garage or shed. A bountiful supply stored in the fall will make the task of starting seeds in the spring an easy one.

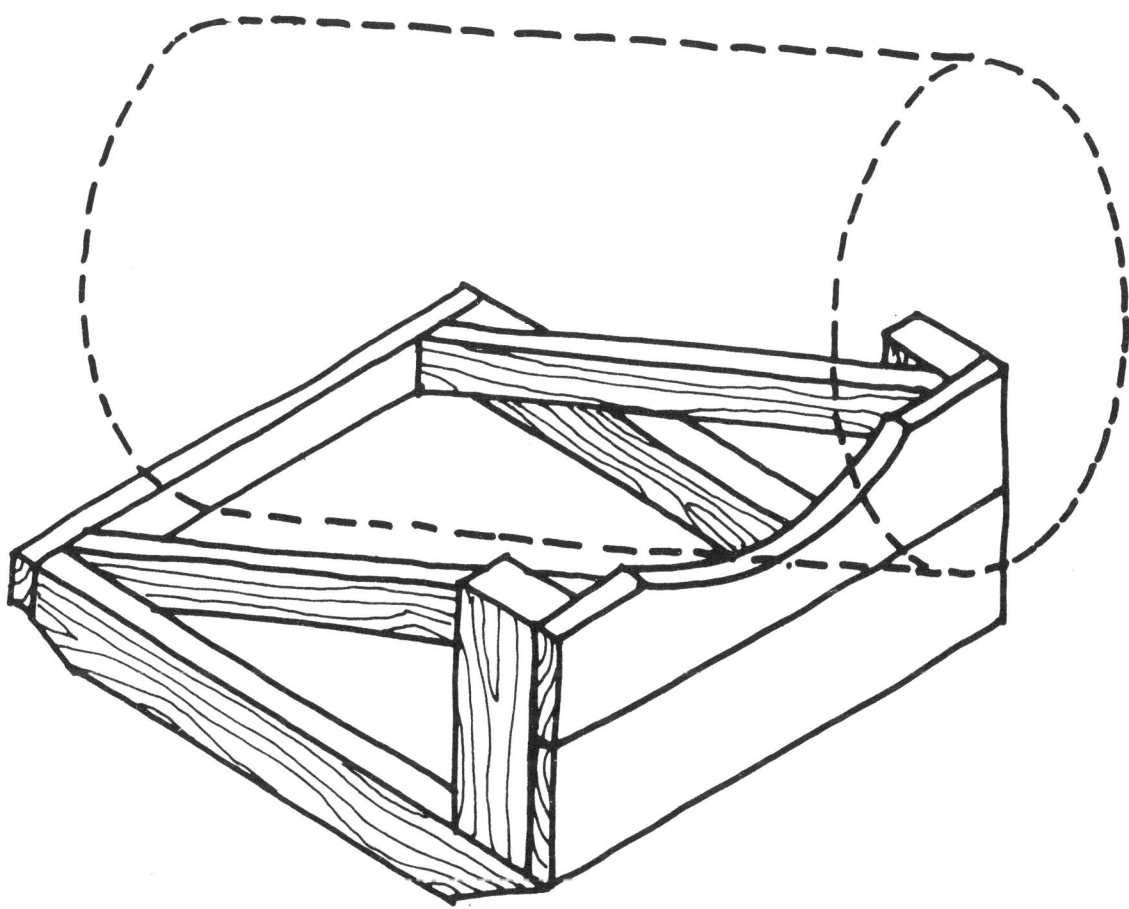

Build a can cradle to hold a 20-gallon metal garbage can or plastic bin. Use the can to store all the materials needed to start tomatoes, peppers, flowers, and more in the spring.

Seedling
Containers,
page 37

Outdoor
Storage Bin,
page 22

Smokehouse,
page 87

Solar Dryer,
page 34

# HARVEST RACK

The sweet sadness of autumn is summed up by the gardener's plight in raising tomatoes in locales with large seasonal temperature swings. Here's how to ripen tomatoes gradually when you have to pick them unripe before the frost.

Most green and slowly reddening tomatoes can be eaten and enjoyed if permitted to ripen gradually. This means in a cool and dark (or at least out of the sun) place, with the tomatoes arranged in such a way that they are not touching. This tomato ripening unit will pay for itself in rescued produce and is fine for other purposes, such as drying onions, beans, seeds, and herbs.

Use 1×4 lumber for building the frame (you'll need fifteen 12-foot 1×4s and six 8-foot 1×4s total). Be careful with those corners—make them square or you'll have trouble fitting the trays. Install 2×4 cleats (you'll need three 10-foot 2×4s and one 5-foot 2×4) about 8 to 10 inches apart to give lots of air space, and place the bottom ones at least 8 inches off the floor. When building shallow trays to hold tomatoes, measure carefully. Trays must run smoothly along the 2×4 cleats yet not be so narrow that they'll fall off. Again, 1×4 lumber is fine for frames. Strengthen each tray with a center piece joining the front and back. Use a fiberglass screen (you'll need 60 square feet) to cover the frame. It is ideal for this, and for drying.

Sort tomatoes as you place them on the frames, with the ripest nearest the front of each tray. This makes future checks on them much easier.

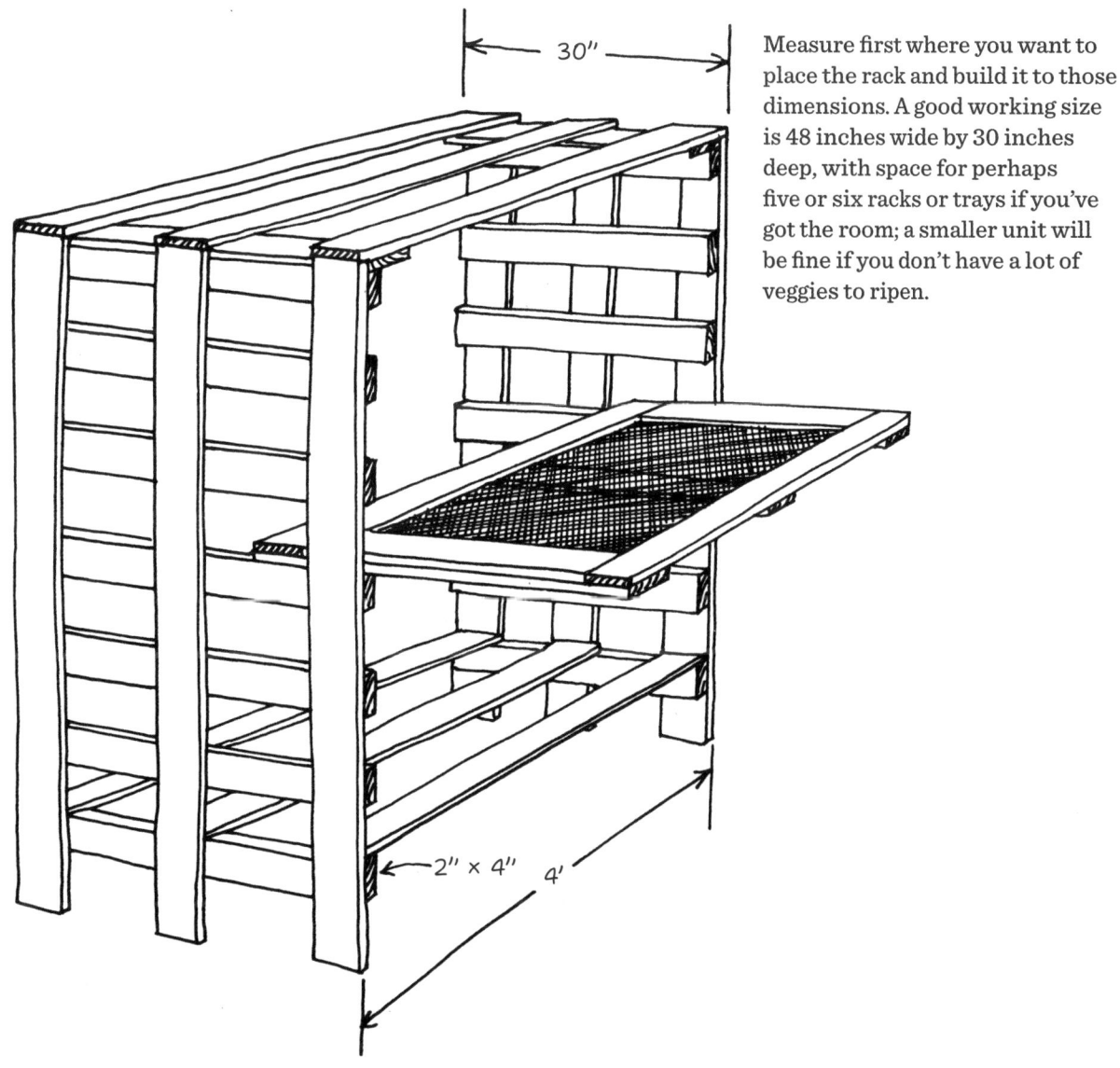

Measure first where you want to place the rack and build it to those dimensions. A good working size is 48 inches wide by 30 inches deep, with space for perhaps five or six racks or trays if you've got the room; a smaller unit will be fine if you don't have a lot of veggies to ripen.

# SOLAR DRYER

In warm, sunny climates, the use of the sun for drying food is practical and inexpensive. Here's a dryer well-suited for fruits and vegetables and is simple to build and easy to use.

This dryer is built around a window sash that is 29″ × 18″. The glass top is sloped to get the most direct rays from the sun. This dryer was built from one 8-foot 2×3 for legs, one 8-foot 1×6 for the tray's side walls, and four 8-foot 1×2s for the tray's braces and supports. The bottom of the tray can be wire screen or boards.

Be sure to wash food thoroughly and keep the solar dryer clean and bug-free to produce safe, high-quality dried foods. Most fruits, vegetables, and herbs are good for drying, but it may take some experimentation to get the technique down. In less favorable climates, it is often possible to do much of the drying in the sun, then place materials in the oven, set at very low heat and with the door left ajar, to complete the drying process.

# LED LIGHT PLANT STAND

If you crave one of those LED-lighted étagères but find their price too high, this unit may be your solution. It is inexpensive to build, provides 16 square feet of growing space, and can be used in many ways.

This unit is excellent for a basement where vegetable plants such as tomatoes, peppers, and cabbages can be started. The lighting units are hung on chains with S-hooks and can easily be shifted to a raised position while you're watering plants or caring for them.

You'll need four 6-foot 2×4 uprights, nine 4-foot 2×2 horizontal pieces, four 4-foot 1×6 sides for plant area, one 4 × 4-foot particleboard or plywood shelf, one 5 × 5-foot plastic sheet shelf covering, two 4-foot LED shop lights with hooks and chains, and one 8-foot 2×2 to be cut into four supports (optional).

Use wood screws throughout. Attach an upper crossbar to each pair of uprights. Build the shelf frame and fasten it at a height comfortable for you. Two top bars are screwed into position 2 feet apart, and steel hooks are screwed into the bars in a position so that the light units hanging from them will be centered properly. Fasten the plywood shelf bottom onto the frame and add the 1×4 side pieces. Plastic sheeting inside the shelf area protects the wood from the damp soil in your planting trays or pots. While most people will use this as a place to start vegetables, it is equally valuable for houseplants.

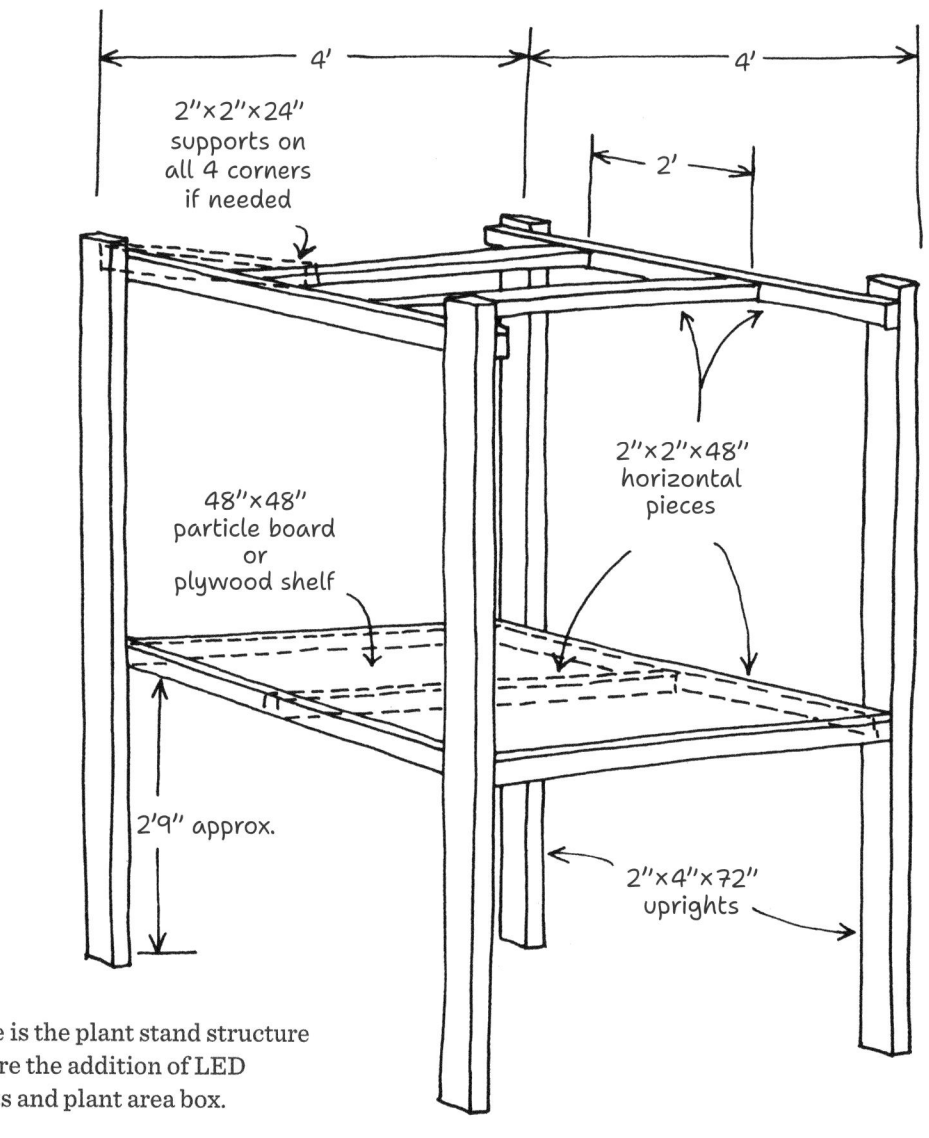

Here is the plant stand structure before the addition of LED lights and plant area box.

# SEEDLING CONTAINERS

The list of containers that can be used for seed-starting is a long one. Here are just a few suggestions. There are many more.

The ideal ones have certain things in common. They are 2½ to 3 inches deep, so that the little seedlings can put down relatively long roots and the soil will not dry out quickly. And they have holes in the bottom, or holes can be punched in them, so the roots are not drowned by overenthusiastic watering and so "bottom watering"—the preferred method for seedlings—is possible.

But for true convenience and long-lasting use, build some flats. Leave a small space for drainage between bottom boards, and place a single layer of newspaper in the flat before it is filled with soil. A board with notches cut at both ends works as a screed to level out the soil after you fill the tray. Can you use scrap lumber to build these? Of course.

tin can

flower pot

peat pot

milk carton

fruit carton

half of 1-gallon plastic jug

aluminum foil pan

# Seedling Flat

A typical seedling flat is 12″ × 18″ × 2¾″. This size is easy to handle, deep enough for root growth, and easily used with peat pots or plant bands for plants that dislike the rigors of transplanting.

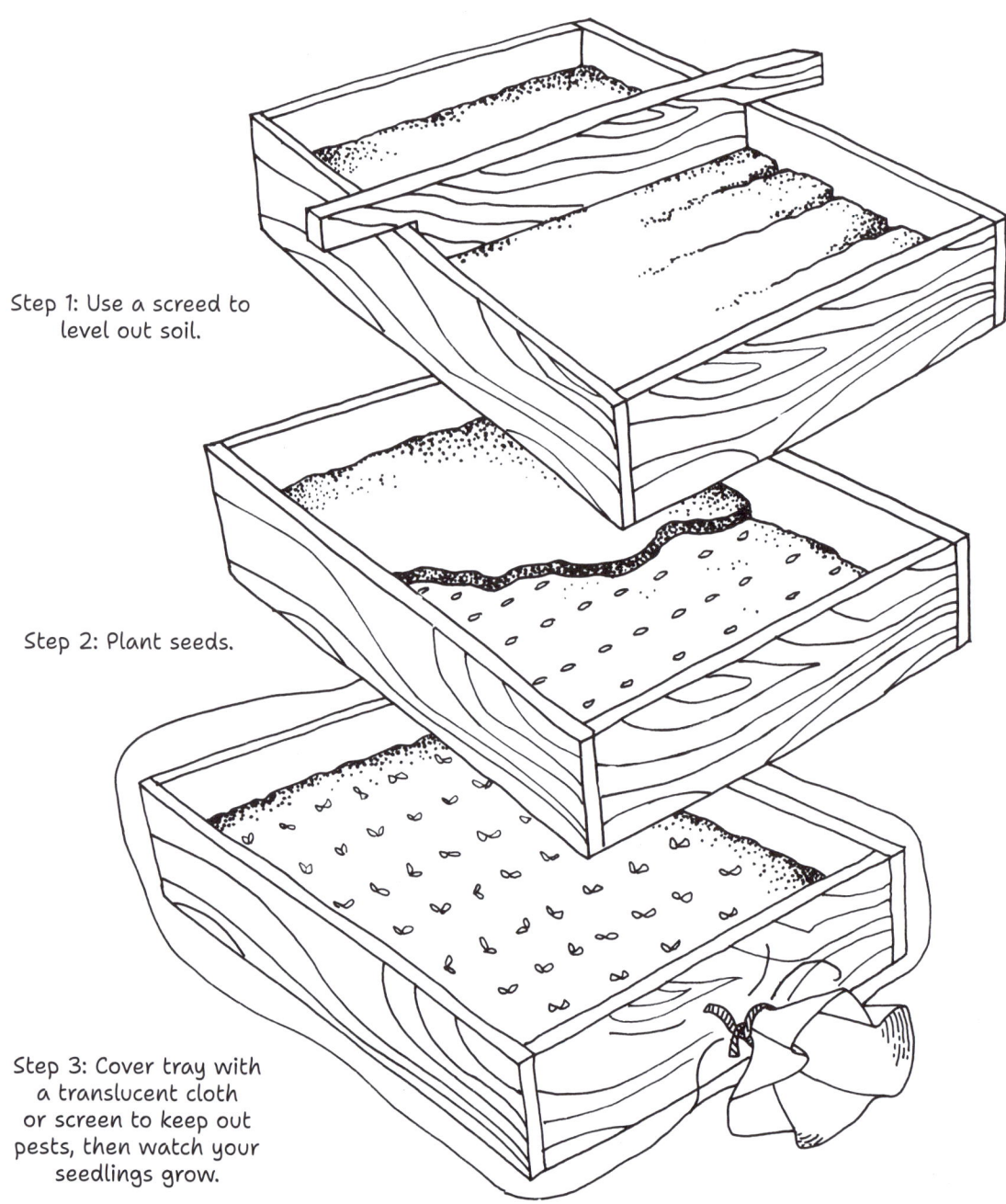

Step 1: Use a screed to level out soil.

Step 2: Plant seeds.

Step 3: Cover tray with a translucent cloth or screen to keep out pests, then watch your seedlings grow.

# PORCH CHAIR

If you've ever had the plastic crack under you as you sat in one of those PVC patio chairs, you'll appreciate the sturdy comfort of this one, with roomy arms that will hold a drink or the book you were reading before you began to nod off.

You might recognize its similarities to the classic Adirondack-style chair, which has been appreciated for its simplicity and clean lines for more than a hundred years.

Choose the type of wood based on your taste and where you expect to use the chair; pine or Douglas fir is fine for a porch chair, but cedar or mahogany is better for a chair that spends time out in the elements. Follow the details closely while cutting the lumber for this one and you'll have no trouble fitting it together.

To make it, you will need one 12-foot 1×3, one 8-foot 1×3, one 14-foot 1×2, one 12-foot 1×8, one 26½-inch 2×2, one 23½-inch 1×6, and one 4-foot 1×4.

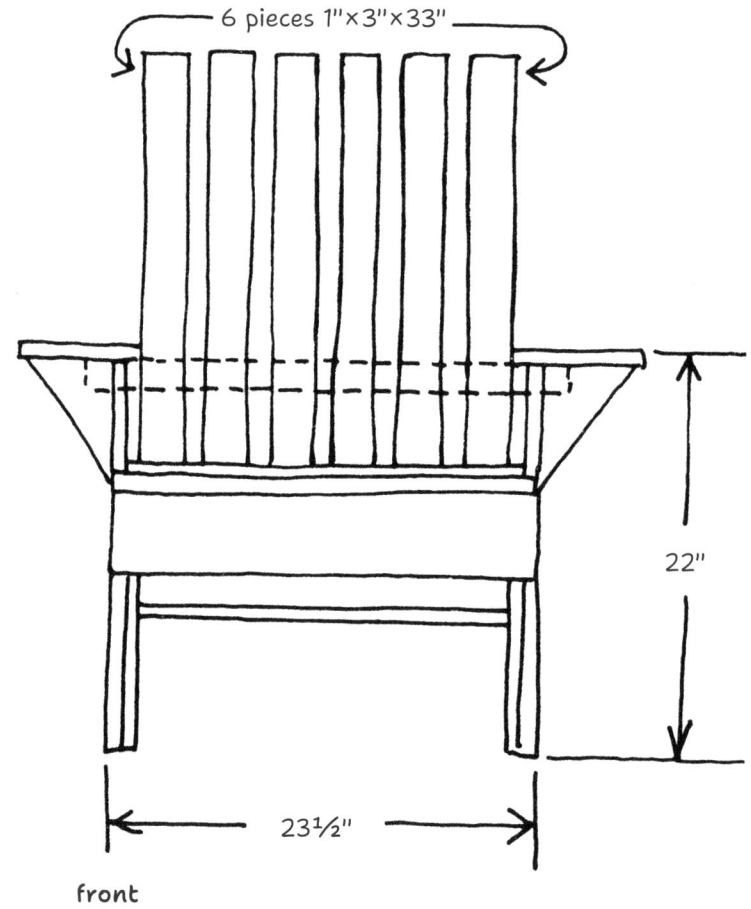

6 pieces 1"×3"×33"

22"

23½"

front

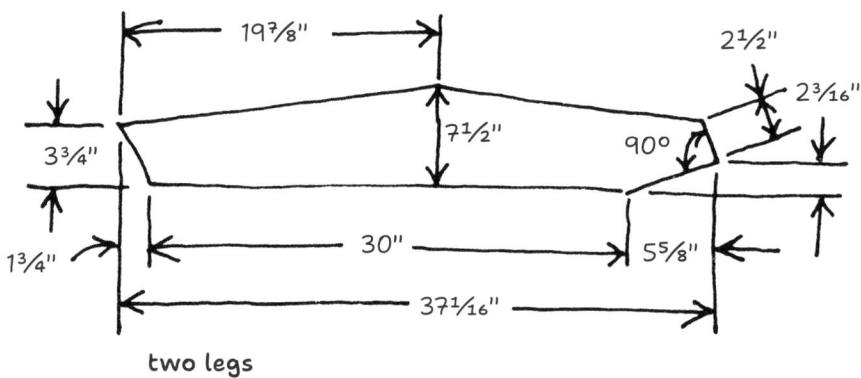

19⅞"

2½"

2³⁄₁₆"

7½"

90°

3¾"

30"

5⅝"

1¾"

37¹⁄₁₆"

two legs

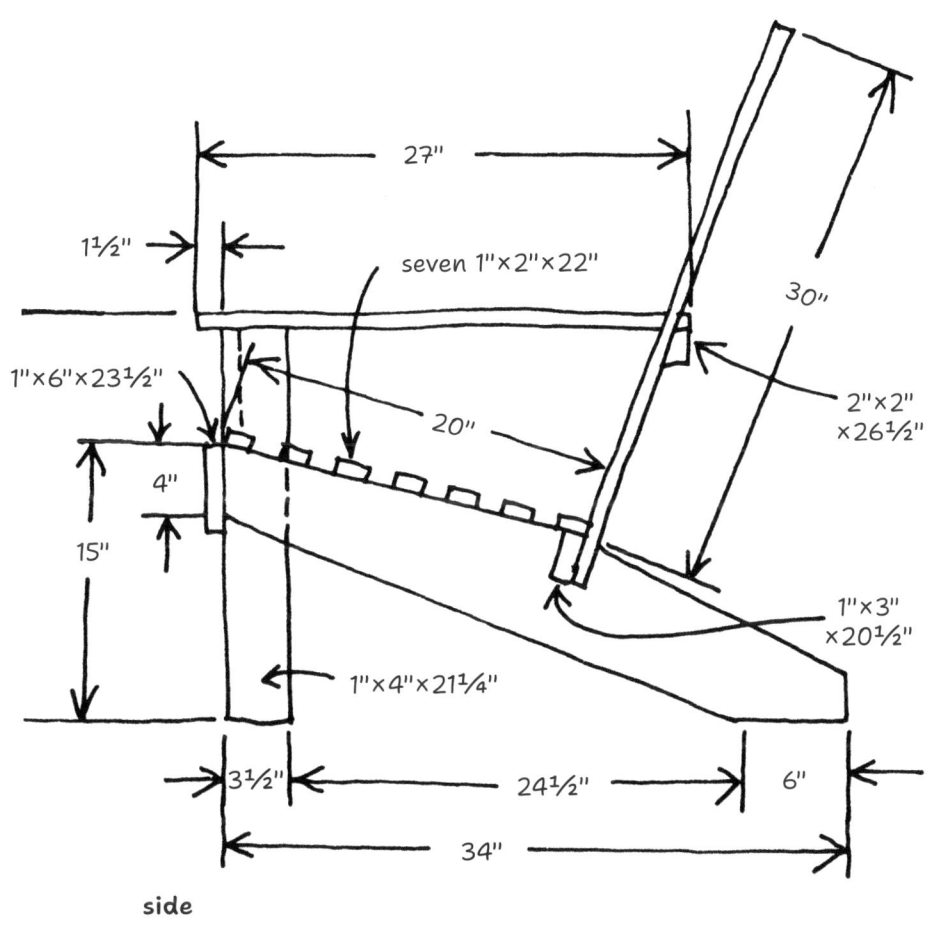

27"

1½"

seven 1"×2"×22"

30"

1"×6"×23½"

20"

2"×2"
×26½"

4"

15"

1"×3"
×20½"

1"×4"×21¼"

3½"

24½"

6"

34"

side

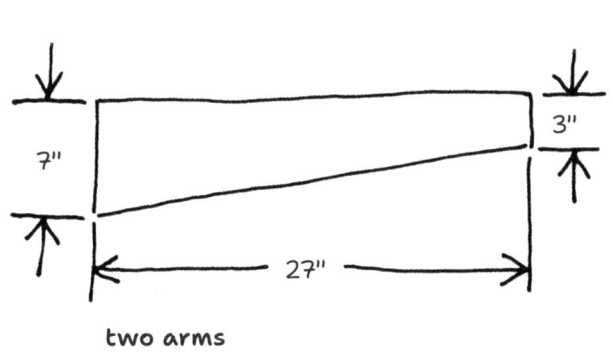

7"

3"

27"

two arms

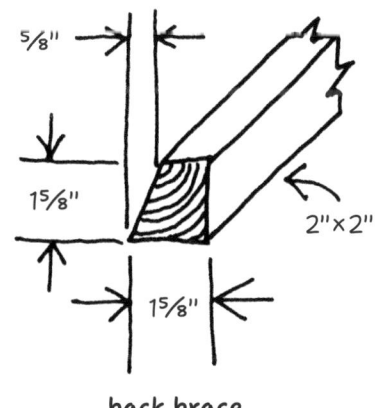

5/8"

1⅝"

2"×2"

1⅝"

back brace

Macramé Hanger, page 48

# MAILBOX HOLDER

If mailbox holders had to be insured, the rates would be high since they are often hit by cars or buried by snowplows. Here's one that could apply for lower insurance rates.

It's set up at an angle that lets it reach out toward the road, and it's swiveled in the center, so it will give a little when hit. And at 3′8″ above the surface of the road, it's at a comfortable level for that mailperson stretching out of their vehicle.

Note carefully that two arms reach out from the post, and that the base for the mailbox is formed by those two arms plus a 2×4 block between them. You'll need one 1″ × 18″ rod or pipe, one 5-foot 4×4, one 3-foot 4×4, one 1-foot 2×4, and one 4-foot 5-inch 1×10.

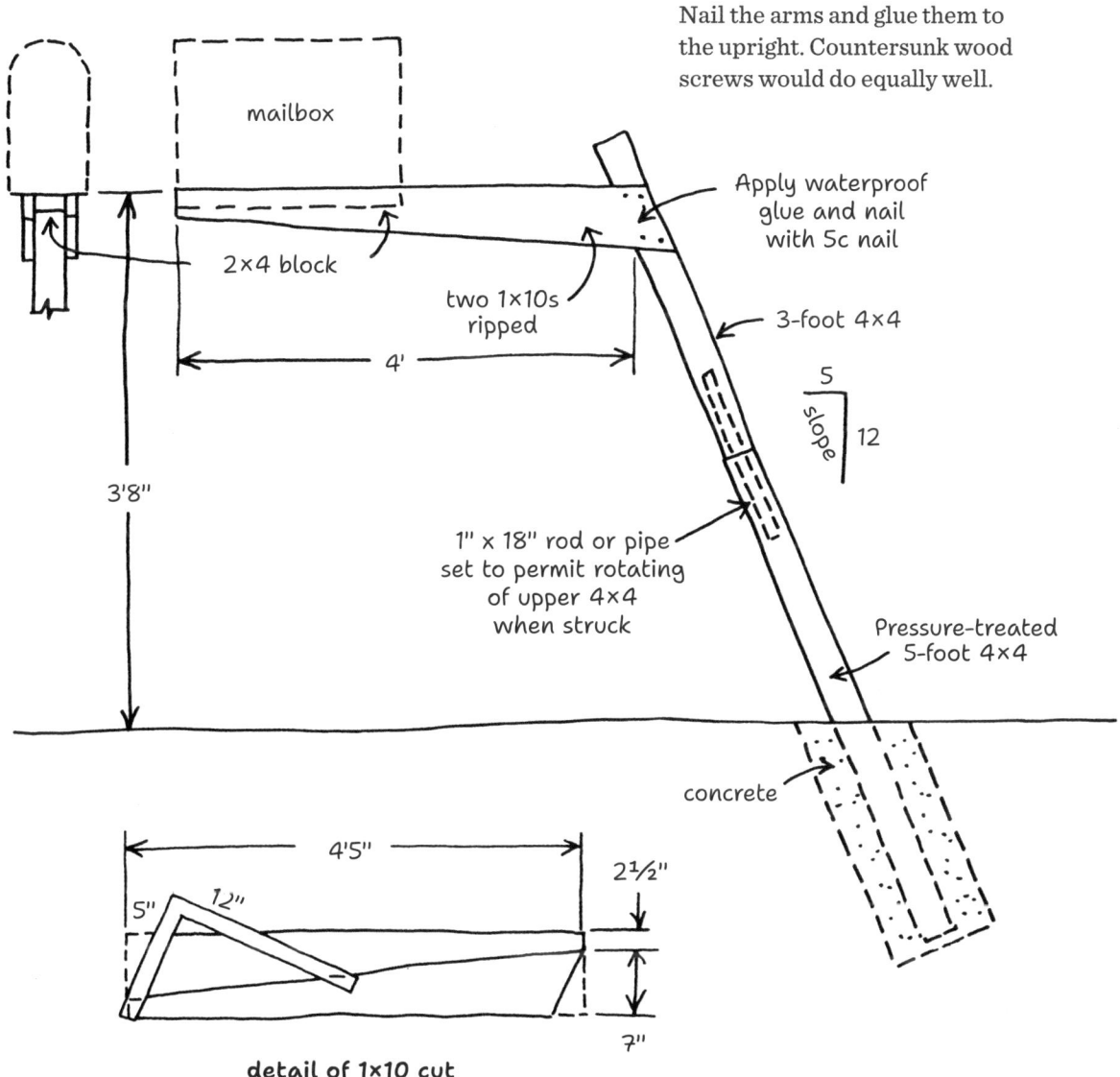

Nail the arms and glue them to the upright. Countersunk wood screws would do equally well.

mailbox

2×4 block

two 1×10s ripped

Apply waterproof glue and nail with 5c nail

3-foot 4×4

4'

slope 5 / 12

3'8"

1" x 18" rod or pipe set to permit rotating of upper 4×4 when struck

Pressure-treated 5-foot 4×4

concrete

4'5"

5"  12"

2½"

7"

detail of 1×10 cut

# HANGING PLANTERS

The most effective planters can be constructed at home, easily and quickly. Here are some ideas—build them as shown or use them as inspiration for your own design.

Shown here is a simple way to create a hanging planter. First find a plastic pot—one of those with the attached saucer. Drill three small holes, spaced the same distance apart, in the saucer lip. Add cord or wire and hang.

How about one with two or three pots, and made of scrap lumber? The size of your pots determines the width of lumber needed. For two 3-inch pots, a 12-inch 1×6 board is good. Cut two holes with a diameter the same size as the pot below its thick upper rim. (Remember back in school how you measured the distance around the pot, divided by 3.14, and got the needed diameter?) Bore one hole in each of the four corners to thread with wire or cord for hanging.

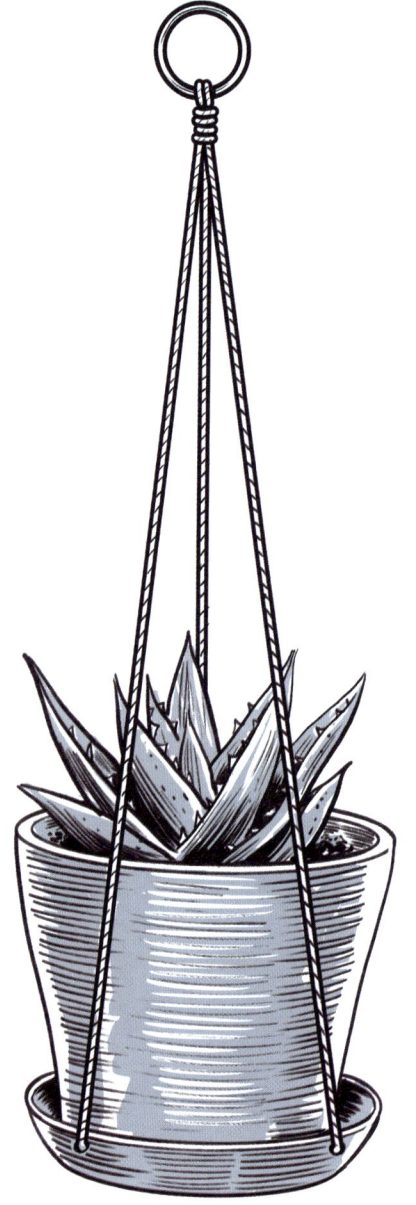

For a lasting job, paint or use waterproof varnish on this double planter. Two pots of Swedish ivy will look great in this.

# MACRAMÉ HANGER

If you can tie a shoestring, you can make this hanger that will hold your plants in style.

You'll need four 6-foot lengths of twine. Baling cord is fine for practice. Use nylon cord if you want your work to last without rotting.

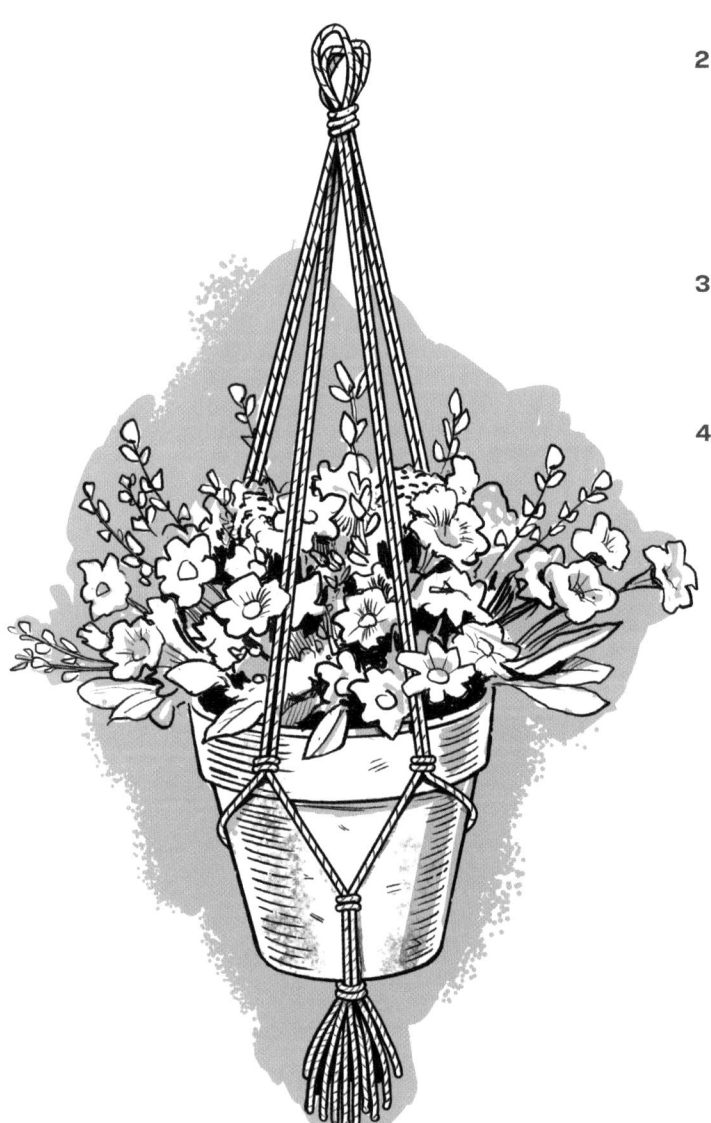

1. Double the cords so all ends are together, then tie a single overhand knot near the folded end of the cords to provide the loop for hanging. Hang the loop over a hook of some kind for easier working.

2. Sort the eight loose ends into four pairs and tie each pair with an overhand knot, halfway between the loop and the end of the strings. Each knot should be the same distance from the ends of the strings. In the illustration you have tied A and B, C and D, E and F, and G and H.

3. Tie overhand knots halfway between those you just tied and the ends of the strings. Tie B and C, D and E, F and G, and H and A, thus achieving a circle.

4. As the final step, gather ends of all strings and tie in one overhand knot, forming a tassel. Your flowerpot sits on that tassel and is surrounded by all those strings.

This can be prettied up by using different-colored cord or adding colored beads above the knots in various ways. And you will quickly learn to adjust the length of the original cords to the size of the pot you wish to hang, with larger pots requiring longer strings.

overhand knot

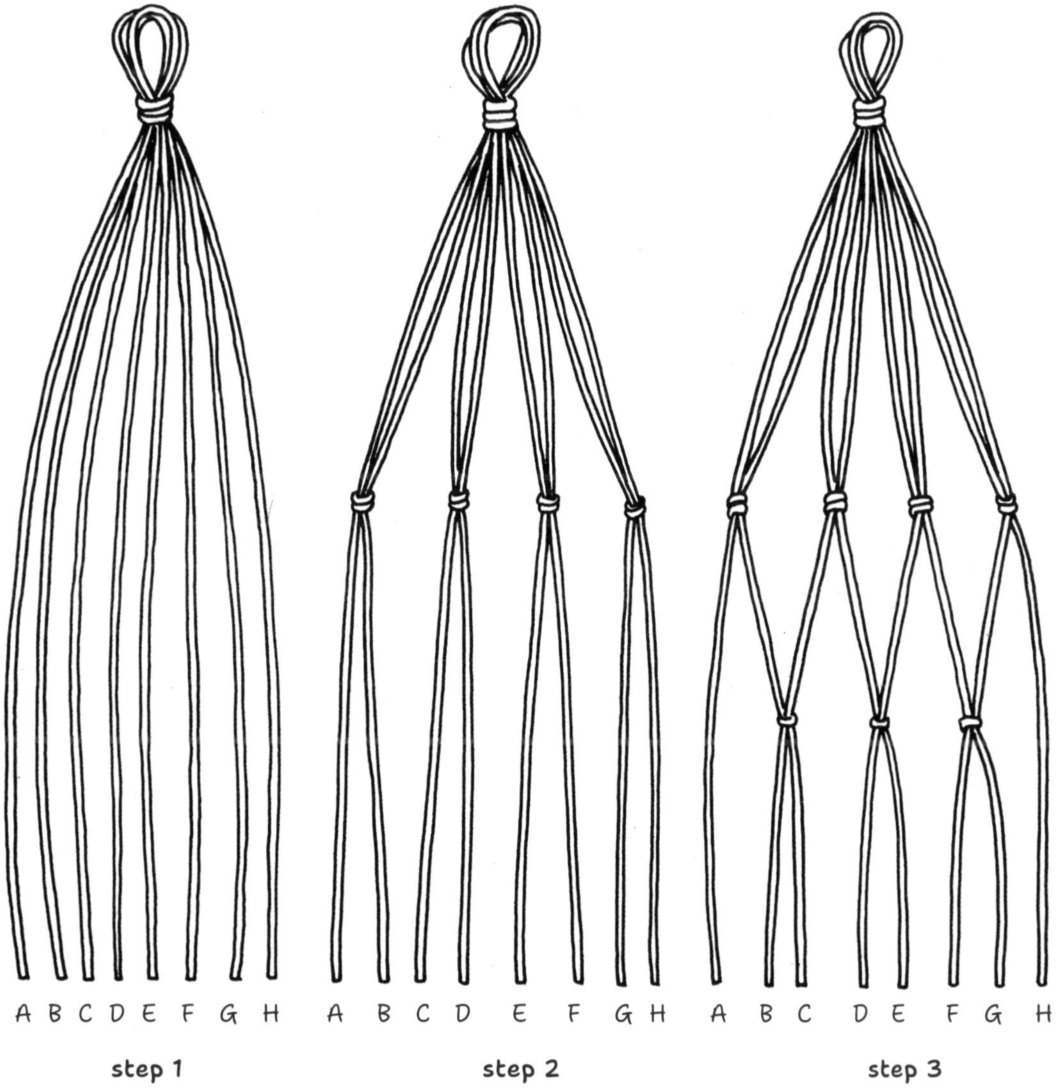

A B C D E F G H

**step 1**

A B C D E F G H

**step 2**

A B C D E F G H

**step 3**

# For the
# Yard & Garden

# Some Notes on Building for the Garden

**You'll find many projects in this section that will make your gardening efforts easier and more rewarding. Just keep in mind that when you're building something that will remain outdoors, you need to use materials that can weather the elements. Keep the following notes in mind.**

## Wood

Most gardening aids can be made of scrap wood or of low-grade lumber, which need not be kiln dried, and other materials readily available from your local hardware store or lumber dealer.

Almost any species of wood is suitable for gardening aids. Softwood is more easily worked, and when ordering from a lumberyard you will get any of a number of species unless you specify a particular one. These would include pine, hemlock, spruce, larch, and fir. The heartwood of cypress, cedar, and redwood is resistant to decay and will cost more.

For gardening purposes, look for the grade of lumber labeled "No. 3 common." Wood can be ordered by the board foot (the equivalent of 12″ × 12″ × 1″ thick) or by linear feet. It is more convenient to estimate the number of linear feet you want for a particular job (48 feet of 1×3 board) and to order it this way than to translate into board feet. Remember also that lumber is specified by nominal dimensions at the time of sawing. Subsequent planing reduces these dimensions. Boards are cut to even foot dimensions: 6, 8, 10, and 12 feet long.

## Lath

Wood lath measures 3/8″ × 1″, comes 4 feet long, and is made of various species. The surfaces are unplaned and it must be handled with care to avoid splinters. Lath is extremely useful around the garden for many purposes.

## Wire

Galvanized steel wire is a good choice because it is long-lasting and easy to find in various thicknesses (a.k.a. gauges). Note: The bigger the gauge number, the thinner the wire.

Don't use copper wire, as copper can be toxic to plants.

## Wire Fabric

Wire fabric is a term used for woven wire products. It is made in mesh sizes starting at 1/2″ × 1/2″ and going up to 4″ × 4″, and in various widths up to 6 feet wide and in rolls up to 100 feet long. Hardware stores and lumber dealers will cut the length you ask for.

## Wire Panels

These are similar to woven wire but are made with thick galvanized steel wire (so thick you could call them rods) welded into various-sized grids. These panels come 3 feet or 4 feet high and in 16-foot lengths. They are rigid enough to bend into freestanding plant supports but can also be hung on posts. Have a bolt cutter or hacksaw handy if you need to cut to a smaller size.

## Fastenings

All fastenings should be non-rusting or galvanized. You will find 6d and 8d nails adequate for most needs. Galvanized wire staples should be used for fastening wire fabric to wood.

# HANDY BOX

This is a handy box to be put up on a post near the entrance of your garden. Fill it with all the little garden tools you use frequently.

It will hold the many things you may currently carry in your pockets, such as string for lining up rows or a favorite trowel, plus the things you find yourself having to go back to the house for—a salt shaker for discouraging the cabbage moths, rubber knee pads needed for fine weeding, a section of old sheeting to be torn up for tomato ties. Make it about mailbox size. If it's too big it will just get cluttered. Save space in it for a notebook with your garden plan and planting schedule, and a pencil to jot down when you planted what and where. Make its roof waterproof with some shingles or a piece of metal flashing. Soon you'll find you're saving many unnecessary steps.

# TOOL SHED

Garden tools need a roof over their heads to protect them from the elements if they are to serve long and well.

If you want something that's easy to obtain and will work well enough, buy one of those prefab metal or plastic sheds that are all too common at big home centers. If you want something a little special, consider this one. It can be finished on the outside so that it either has the same exterior as your home or blends well with it.

Note that it is built on 4×6 pressure-treated skids. While this means it can be moved, such a move isn't something you will want to try every day, as the finished product is heavy. The other benefit of building this on skids is that the floor is raised well off the ground, virtually eliminating the problem of moisture gradually eating away the bottom of the building—though it's still a good idea to make the floor out of pressure-treated plywood. An alternative is to build the shed on a concrete block base, but with pressure-treated pieces on the bottoms of the walls.

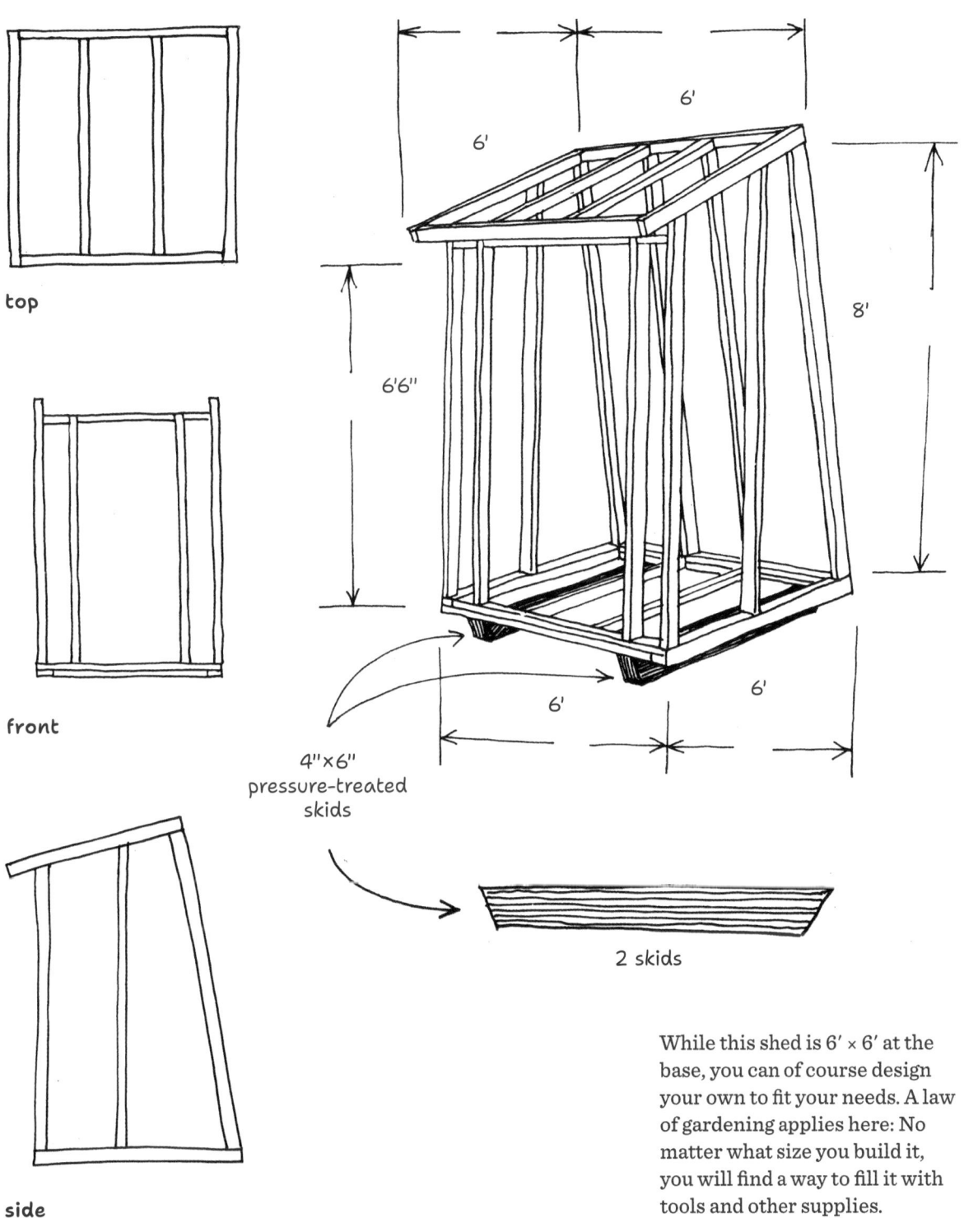

**top**

**front**

**side**

6'

6'

6'6"

8'

6'

6'

4"×6"
pressure-treated
skids

2 skids

While this shed is 6′ × 6′ at the base, you can of course design your own to fit your needs. A law of gardening applies here: No matter what size you build it, you will find a way to fill it with tools and other supplies.

# TOOL STORAGE

Gardening chores are completed much more quickly and in a better frame of mind if tools are readily available in this handy tool storage.

If a hunt for a hoe must precede hoeing the peas, the work becomes a chore. No better way to avoid such troubles than by creating a place for each tool. Two options are offered here: One is a professional, efficient, and long-lasting storage rack, and the other is a simpler alternative.

As seen in the illustration below, you can either drill large holes with a hole saw and complete the notches with a handsaw, or you could cut each notch entirely with a jigsaw. Fasten the rack pieces to the wall with angle brackets or a thin wooden cleat.

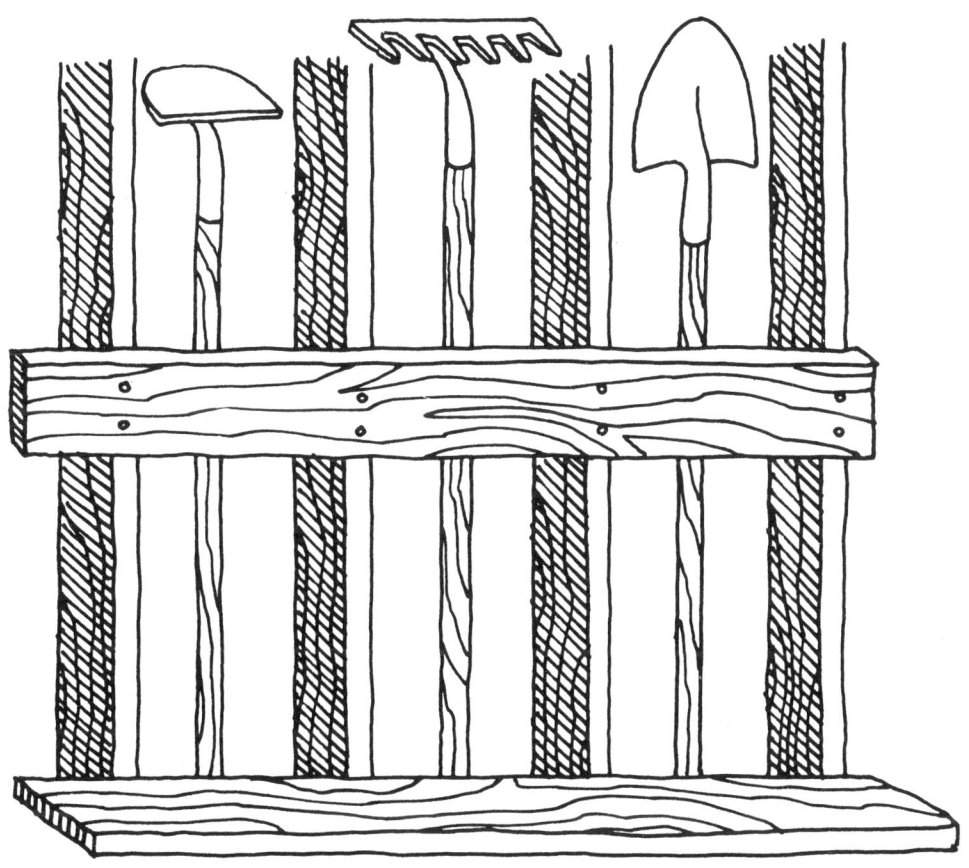

In this simpler alternative to the storage at left, a piece of lumber nailed across the studs of a garage or barn has the sole virtue of being quick to achieve.

# HOSE STORAGE

Anyone who has ever put away a hose knows how frustrating they can be to roll up without getting kinks. Here are some solutions.

The simplest way to store a hose is to hammer a big spike into the studding of your barn or garage and hang it up there. It's also the surest way to ensure its early demise. Take a few minutes and install supports that will permit the hose to be hung in large circles without kinking. The illustrations show several ways to do this. You may think of others.

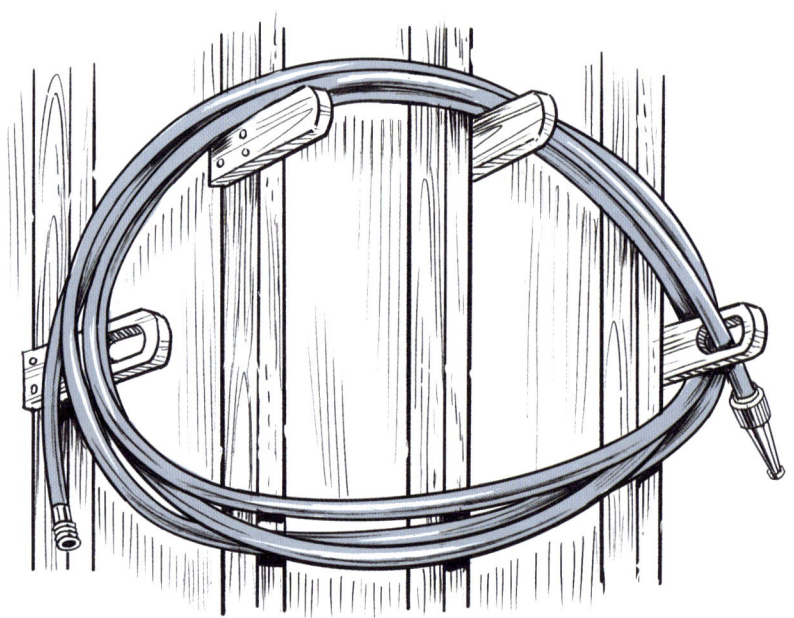

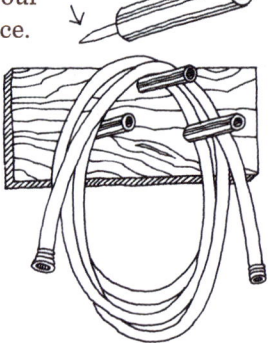

Three spikes covered with old hose will hold your new hose in place.

A piece of tire tacked over an arm will do the job.

# COLD FRAMES

Imagine moving your garden three to four hundred miles south each spring and fall. That's about what a cold frame or hotbed can do for your gardening effort. By using one or both of them you can extend your growing season 4 to 6 weeks on each end.

Beginners should start with a cold frame. It's cheaper both to build and, unless the old fermenting-manure heating method is used, easier to operate than a hotbed. And it's a good teacher. You will quickly learn the tricks of controlling this tiny environment to your advantage.

Some gardening books will tell you to build frames of concrete or concrete block. This is fine, but only if you are absolutely sure of your site and of the size you want. Better to build first with wood so that any error can be rectified easily.

Start modestly, with a single 6 × 8-foot bed. This will give you the feel of working with a cold frame and its possibilities in your area. Such a modest beginning, too, will give you valuable insight into the correct location and construction of more ambitious frames, tailored to your location and needs.

Here are some basic points about the design, construction, and use of the cold frame.

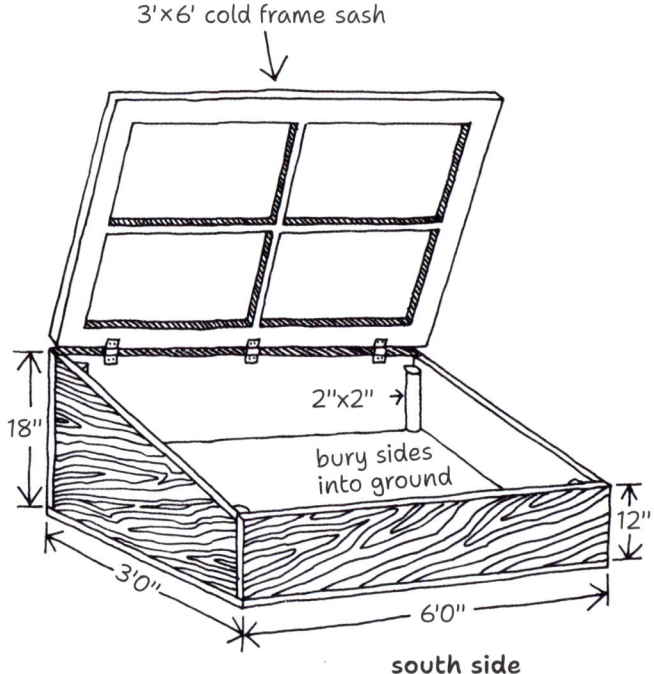

3'×6' cold frame sash

18"

2"x2"

bury sides into ground

12"

3'0"

6'0"

**south side**

Here is a good model to begin with. It's simple to build and small enough so that even a short-armed person can reach into all areas of it, but large enough to help in your gardening.

## Building the Frame

You can use 2×4s for the corner stakes, though in most cases 2×2s will provide enough strength without intruding as much into the cold frame area. For the frame itself, get 1″ × 12″ rough lumber or 2×12 boards. Pressure-treated lumber is durable and affordable, while cedar or cypress would provide a balance of longevity and good looks, but at a high price. Cheap Douglas fir framing lumber will hold up to the elements better than you might expect, and it can be protected from the soil with some plastic sheeting to last even longer.

Find or purchase a sash, then build the frame to fit it. A frame that is 18 inches high in rear and 12 inches high in front is ideal, both for permitting the runoff of rainfall and for maximum sun in the cold frame.

## Building the Sash

There are several possibilities. The easiest but most expensive option is to purchase it. Standard sizes are 3×6, 3×3, and 2×4. Another possibility is to use old storm windows, which are usually cheap and available and are usually 2½′ × 4½′. The third possibility is to build your own, using rigid acrylic or polycarbonate sheets (a.k.a. Plexiglas), which is much more durable than the thin plastic sheeting that is often used.

## Amending Soil

If your soil is rich, simply place the cold frame where you want it, in a slight trench so the bottom of the frame is at least 1 inch below the surface. But if conditions are less than ideal, dig out a 1-foot layer from the site. If drainage may be a problem, put down a 3-inch base of gravel, top that with 1 or 2 inches of peat moss, then add a layer of rich soil and compost that will bring the site back to grade. Pull soil up around the outer sides for improved insulation.

## Planting

In the spring, when the cold frame will get its greatest use, there are several methods to experiment with. One is to plant hardy vegetables and flowers directly in the cold frame soil. This can be done with lettuce, cabbages and their relatives, and other hardy types.

Another method is to seed these into flats, then place the flats in the cold frames. Yet another is used with heat-loving plants such as tomatoes, peppers, and eggplants. These can be started under lights indoors or in a hotbed, then transplanted into peat pots and later transferred to the cold frame for hardening off before going into the garden. A beauty of the cold frame is its adaptability to anyone's gardening habits.

When seeding directly into the cold frame soil, make rows only 1 or 2 inches apart, thin ruthlessly, and move plants out and into the garden before they are competing for sunlight and growing room, becoming weakened in the process.

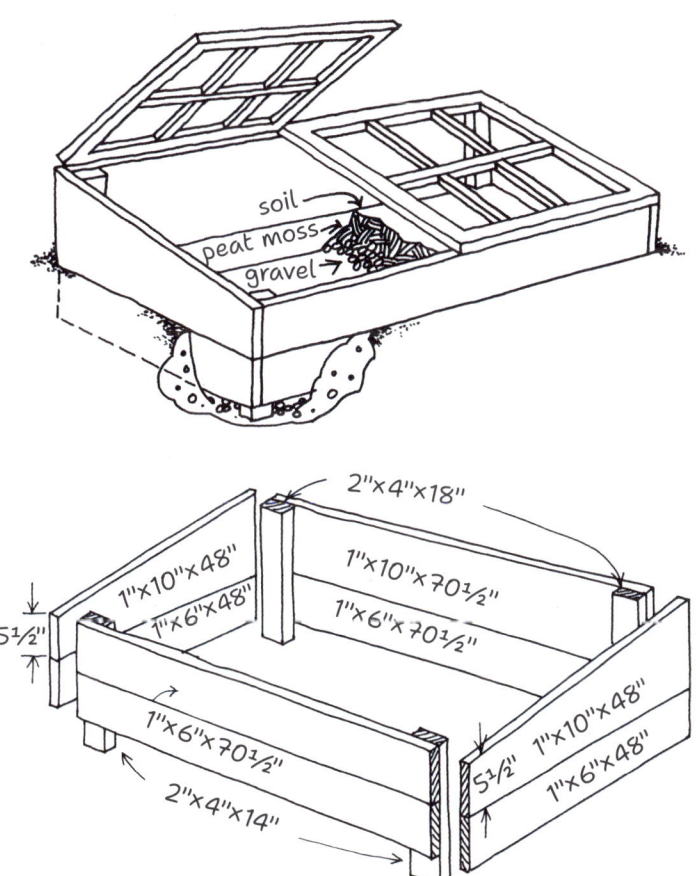

These two diagrams show another cold frame that is easy to construct using two 3 × 4-foot storm sashes. Use loose pin hinges to make it easier to remove the sash for repainting or when not in use.

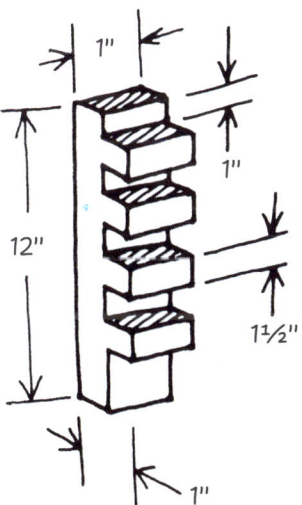

Use this block for holding up the sash.

If you move plants (such as tomatoes in peat pots) to the cold frame, it is a good idea to cushion them on a blanket of compost or peat moss that is well dampened. The plants will quickly push roots out through the sides of the pots and into the moss, providing an even stronger network of roots when the plants are moved into the garden.

While the cold frame is a busy place in early spring, it should not be left idle the remainder of the year. Left open in summer, it is a good place for starting plants that will be moved into the garden when other crops are harvested. In the fall, it can be used to grow a family's lettuce supply, for example, or to delight you with an always-available supply of those hardy and handy herbs, chives and parsley.

## Regulating Temperature

What do you do when the cold frame is full of young plants and the weather report calls for frost with possible snow? Bundle it up, following your carefully laid plans of weeks ago. Blanket the frame. Use canvas or burlap or fiberglass batts, roofing paper with a layer of pine needles, or heavy plastic. If you use such a blanket, have a system that will hold it in place no matter how the winds roar. You can screw a heavy hook into each corner of the cold frame and use them to tie the blanket in place. When weather continues to be cold and cloudy, this can be left in place for several days without harming the plants.

The danger of heat and dehydration, however, is far greater than the danger of cold, even during the early spring and late fall when you will be using your cold frame the most. Remember that even on the coldest winter day, the bright sun can quickly push the temperature in the cold frame up to above 80°F (27°C), which should be the maximum. Provide a system of props so the sash can be raised if there is a chance of overheating. Unless prevailing winds blow directly into the cold frame, there is little danger of damaging plants through chilling them.

The most foolproof way of regulating temperature is to install automatic cold-frame lifting mechanisms that prevent the need to constantly monitor and manually open and close the top when temperatures fluctuate in spring. These devices have a type of wax inside a piston that expands when it gets hot, so they're a low-tech and reasonably affordable solution.

## Watering

You will be surprised how much more water plants in a cold frame will require. Think of this when selecting the site. Tepid water is a must for tiny plants, and it must be applied in a fine mist or spray, not hosed on.

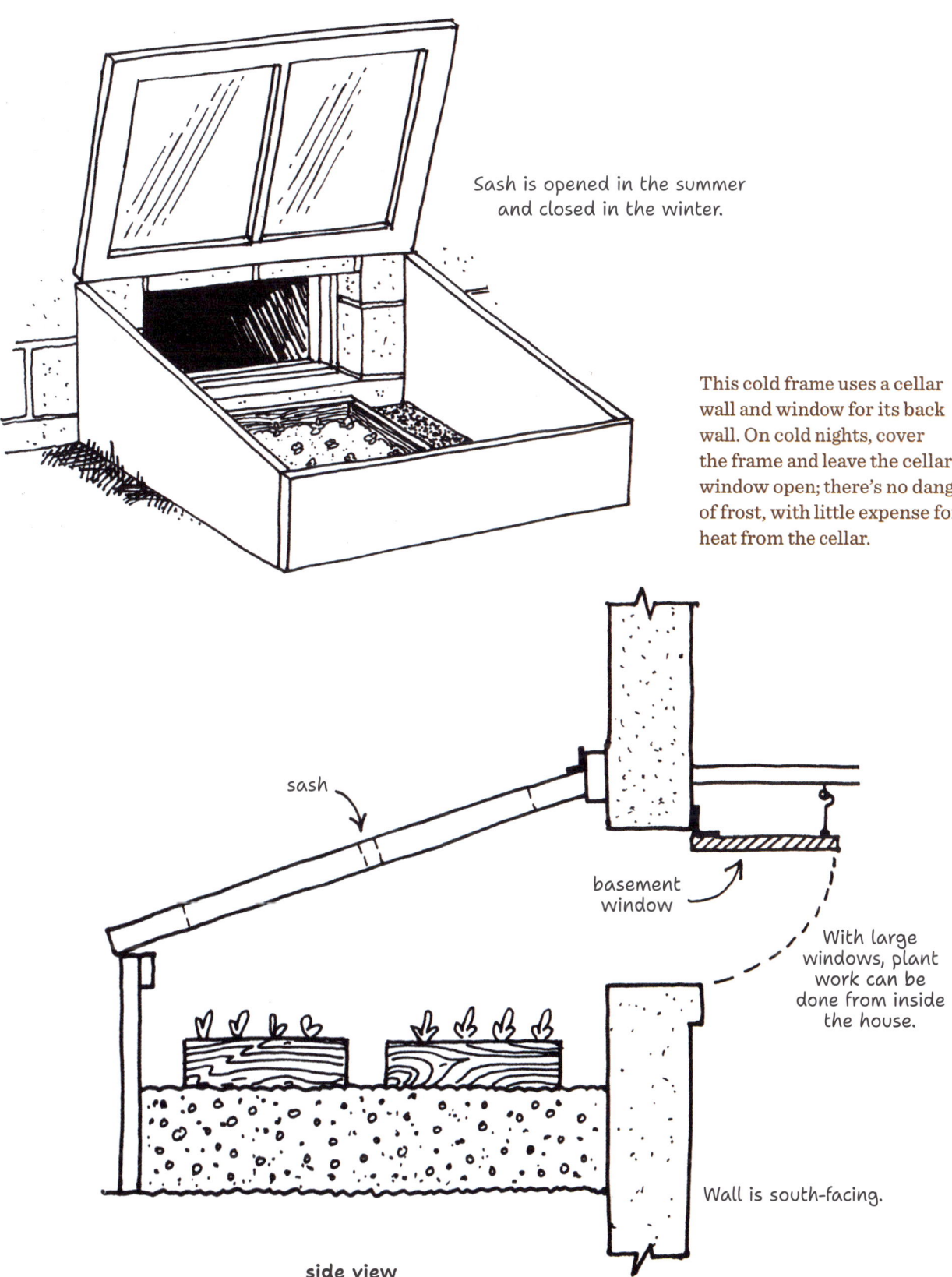

Sash is opened in the summer
and closed in the winter.

This cold frame uses a cellar
wall and window for its back
wall. On cold nights, cover
the frame and leave the cellar
window open; there's no danger
of frost, with little expense for
heat from the cellar.

sash

basement
window

With large
windows, plant
work can be
done from inside
the house.

Wall is south-facing.

**side view**

# HOTBEDS

The cold frame, developed centuries ago, could be called a solar-heated device to give it a modern touch. Add any other source of heat and you have a hotbed.

## Manure Hotbeds

The original way to provide heat was to put a deep layer of fermenting manure under the soil. With electricity much more expensive today, you might consider trying it if you have an available supply of chicken, horse, or cow manure.

For a single-sash 3 × 6-foot bed, you need a cubic yard of fresh manure, with one-third of it straw or other litter. Pile it 10 to 12 days in advance and dampen it if it is dry. In 4 to 5 days it should be heating. Turn the pile, getting outer materials into the center where they will also heat up. In 4 to 5 more days it should be ready.

Dig 2 feet down on the hotbed site and remove all soil. The sides of the hotbed should be built wide enough to fit to the bottom of this excavation. Put the hotbed into place, then shovel in 18 inches of manure, building it in layers which should be packed down. On top of this place the soil, 6 inches deep if you plan to plant directly into it, or 2 inches deep if you will place containers on it. In winter, mound soil or sawdust against the frame. Manure should continue to generate heat for at least 2 weeks. To make a larger bed double this size, see plans at right.

It is difficult to control temperature since there is no relationship between the heat desired and the heat generated.

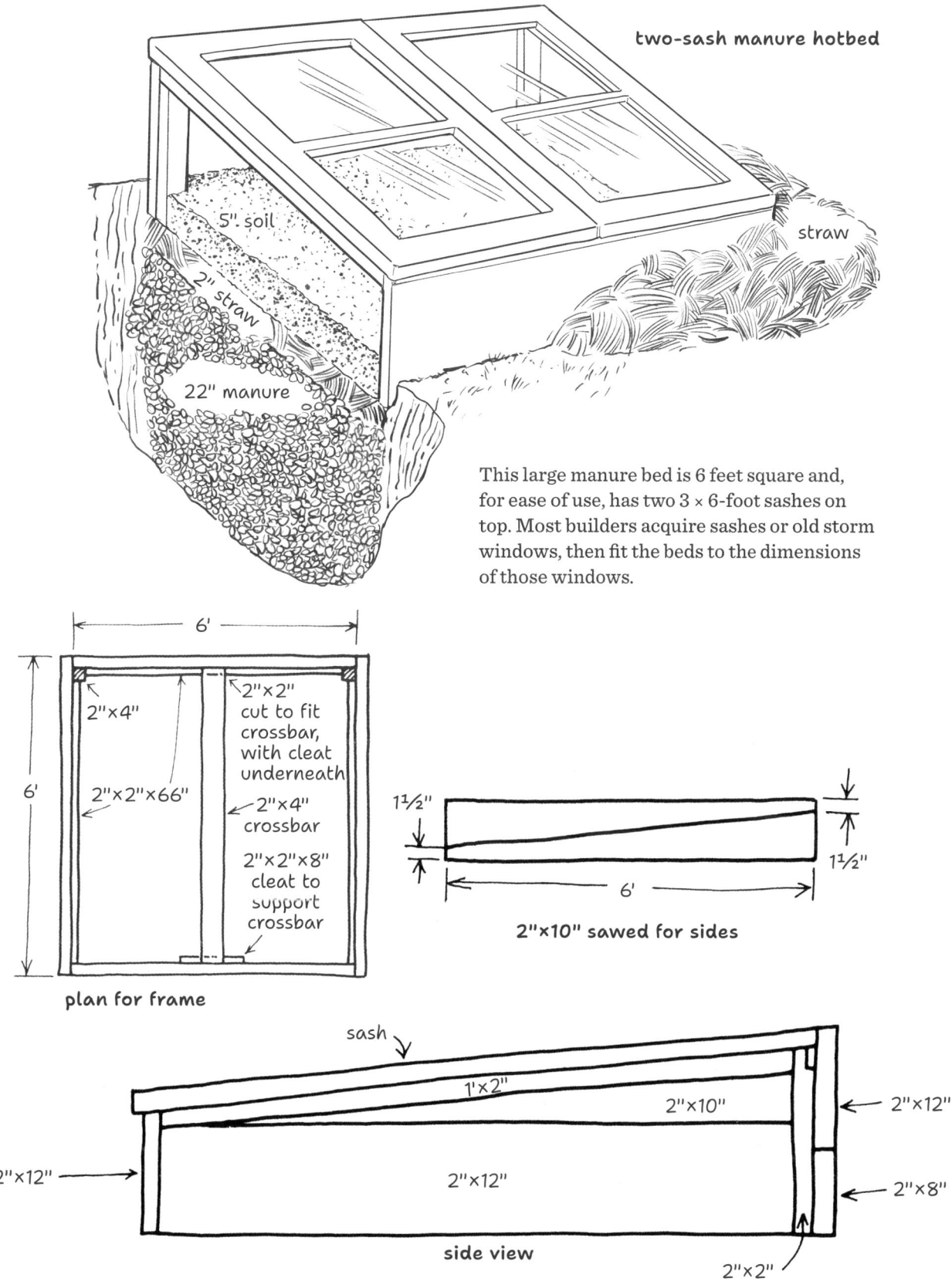

**two-sash manure hotbed**

5" soil

2" straw

22" manure

straw

This large manure bed is 6 feet square and, for ease of use, has two 3 × 6-foot sashes on top. Most builders acquire sashes or old storm windows, then fit the beds to the dimensions of those windows.

6'

6'

2"×4"

2"×2"×66"

2"×2" cut to fit crossbar, with cleat underneath

2"×4" crossbar

2"×2"×8" cleat to support crossbar

**plan for frame**

1½"

1½"

6'

**2"×10" sawed for sides**

sash

1'×2"

2"×10"

2"×12"

2"×12"

2"×12"

2"×8"

2"×2"

**side view**

## Electric Hotbeds

Other sources of heat are electricity, from light bulbs or thermostatically controlled electric cable, and, in elaborate hotbeds, from hot-water pipes and steam.

For the beginner, we recommend electric soil heating cable, which is thermostatically controlled, thus promising constant temperature and a saving of electricity. The 50-foot cable length should be adequate for the 3 × 6-foot bed, but this should be checked against the recommendations of manufacturers of specific cables.

Install electric cable carefully for the most efficient operation and lowest electricity costs. Excavate about 20 inches of soil from the site and build sides of the hotbed to reach down to this depth for insulation. To assure proper drainage, put down a foot-deep layer of crushed gravel. Top this with 2 or 3 inches of sand or vermiculite for a bed for the cable. Now loop the cable along the bed, keeping it about 3 inches from the edges and making certain it does not cross over on itself. On top of this place a sheet of either hardware cloth or wire screen with a fine mesh. This will assist in spreading the heat evenly in the bed. Then add 4 to 6 inches of soil. Be sure to keep an eye on plants right after they are placed in the hotbed since this is when they are most vulnerable.

## Controlling Temperature and Humidity

The chief dangers of hotbeds are overheating, drying out, and damping off. Overheating can happen so quickly on a sunny day that you should only operate these beds if someone is home all day. You must raise the sash to let the heat escape, and you need to water the bed with tepid water more than once daily. At the same time, if the air and soil are too damp and the air is warm and humid, conditions are ideal for damping off, a seedling-killing condition caused by various fungi. Again, this risk can be avoided by opening the sash to provide fresh air.

The more heat you can conserve, the lower your energy expense. Thus it is a good idea to blanket the glass each night to minimize the loss of heat.

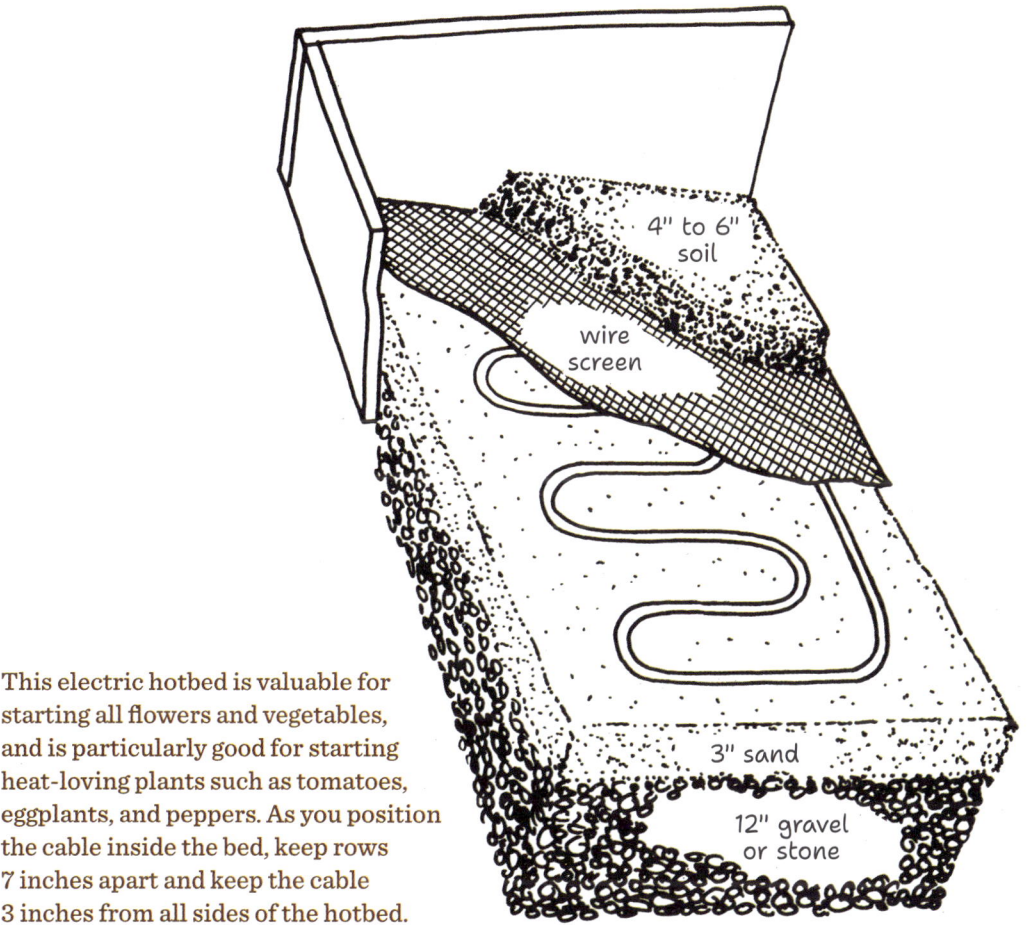

4" to 6" soil

wire screen

3" sand

12" gravel or stone

This electric hotbed is valuable for starting all flowers and vegetables, and is particularly good for starting heat-loving plants such as tomatoes, eggplants, and peppers. As you position the cable inside the bed, keep rows 7 inches apart and keep the cable 3 inches from all sides of the hotbed.

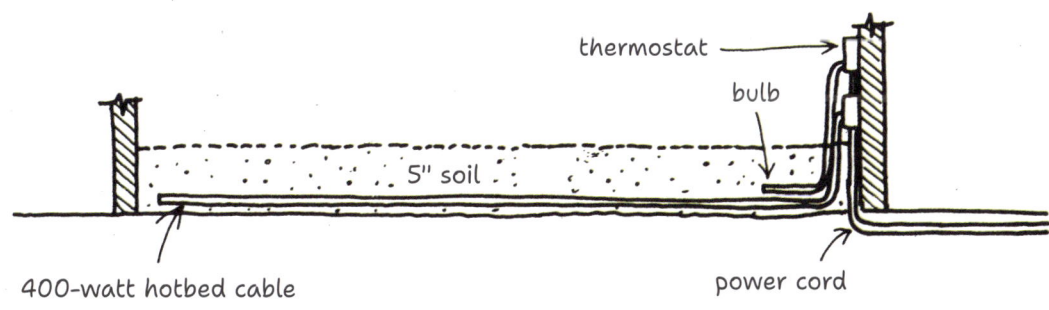

thermostat

bulb

5" soil

400-watt hotbed cable

power cord

**side view of electric hotbed**

Plant
Supports,
page 95

Plant
Protectors,
page 76

Compost Bin, page 70

Cold Frames, page 59

Seedling Containers, page 37

# COMPOST BINS

Every organic gardener relies on compost for healthy, hardy plants. House it in one of these handy bins and use as a soil amendment or as a mulch.

The construction of bins ranges from staking up circles of chicken wire to the careful building of concrete block or brick structures. The simplest is often the best. That circle of mesh provides aeration and is easy to move when you wish to turn the pile and speed its decay.

To make the bin shown below, find some strong wire mesh—4 or 5 feet wide is good. Cut a section 9 feet long. Wire the two ends together, forming a circle. Fill it with composting material. When it's time to turn the pile, remove the wire, set it beside the pile, then fork the pile back into the wire frame, remembering of course to place the outer, uncomposted material into the center of the pile this time.

For fast results, build a series of three bins, using chicken wire or a heavier mesh. This permits you to start the compost in one pile, turn it over into the next, and finish it in the third, meanwhile starting other piles in the first bin. Such a continuous process will speed and increase compost production.

In the following pages are some other bins to consider. No matter which bin you decide to make, here are some points to remember.

### Composting Guidelines

1. **The ideal size** is 6 feet wide, 3 to 5 feet high, and any length beyond 6 feet.
2. **Walls should not exclude air**, or the aerobic (with air) bacterial action of breaking down the organic matter will be halted.
3. **Place the pile close to the garden**, which is the source for much of the composting material and where most of the compost will be used. A shady spot near a water supply is ideal.
4. **Compost as much material as you can find**, following the order and depth of materials in the illustration at right for good results. The pile will shrink to about half its original size—there's no such thing as too much compost.

## Compost Materials Stacked in Order

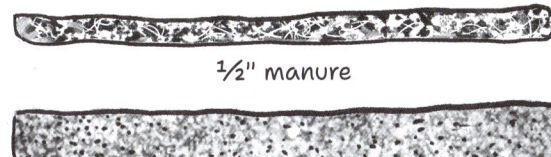
½" manure

1" soil or sand

6–12" organic refuse

water

½" manure

1" soil or sand

6–12" organic refuse

# Two-Bin Composting

This two-bin container is both practical and long-lived. Concrete blocks are held in place with mortar or construction adhesive (you can build it much faster with adhesive than with mortar), and the blocks are set on edge with the holes open to allow free passage of air. Boards are put in place as the pile builds up. The best use for this model would be to build up a pile in the first bin, let it "cook" for several weeks, then shovel it into the second bin for final composting while building up another pile in the first bin.

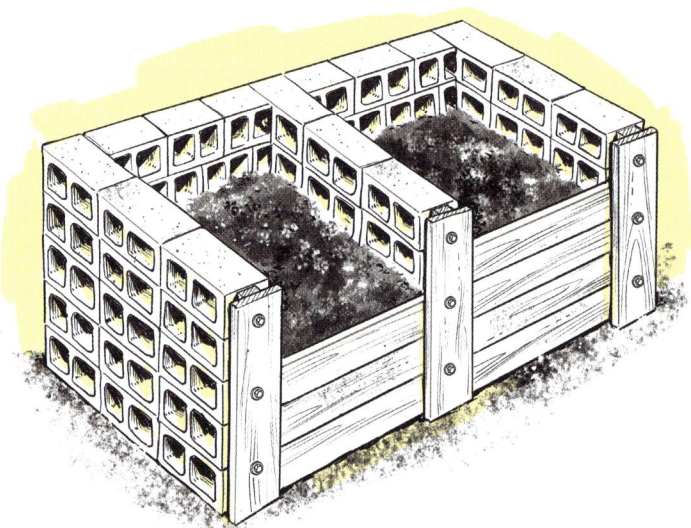

# New Zealand Compost Box

This box requires two 10-foot 2×2s (to be cut into six 39-inch 2×2s) plus twelve 8-foot 1×6s (to be cut into twenty-four pieces, each 48 inches long). Pressure-treated wood would be the most durable, but if you want to avoid chemically treated wood, cedar is the next best thing. Douglas fir and hemlock will hold up okay for temporary structures above ground.

The uprights are dug 3 inches into the ground and the sideboards are spaced a half-inch apart to permit air circulation. The front boards, which slide in and out, make the work of filling and emptying the box much easier. If you use longer uprights and more side pieces, you can build a higher pile.

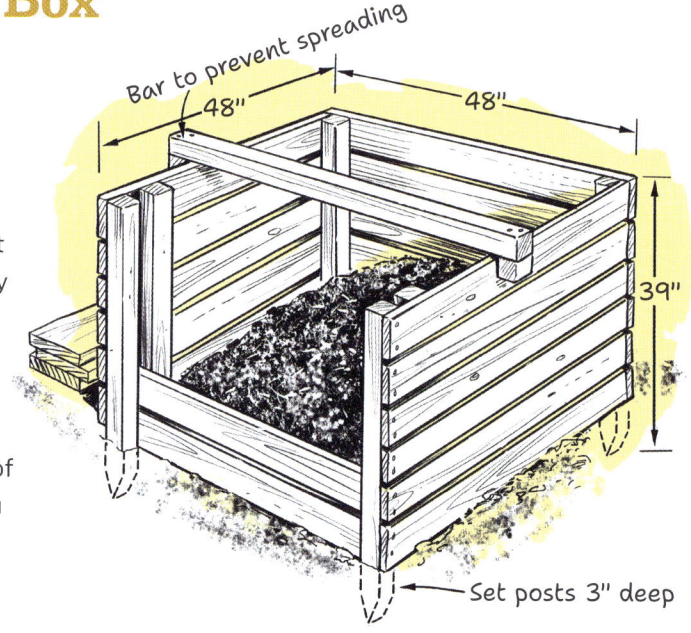

Bar to prevent spreading

48"

48"

39"

Set posts 3" deep

# Handy Composter

Here is an easy bin to assemble and reassemble. Using eight 10-foot 2×2s or similar wood, make four frames, each 4 feet high and 6 feet wide. Reinforce the corners with 2×2s as shown. Cover each frame with chicken wire (you'll need 96 square feet)—the ½-inch mesh will hold its shape longer than the cheaper and larger meshes.

Link these panels into two L-shaped sections and use screen-door hooks to link into a square, or use two screen-door hooks at each corner rather than forming the L-shaped sections. When the pile needs to be turned, take the sides apart, reassemble it beside the compost pile, and fork the pile back into the bin.

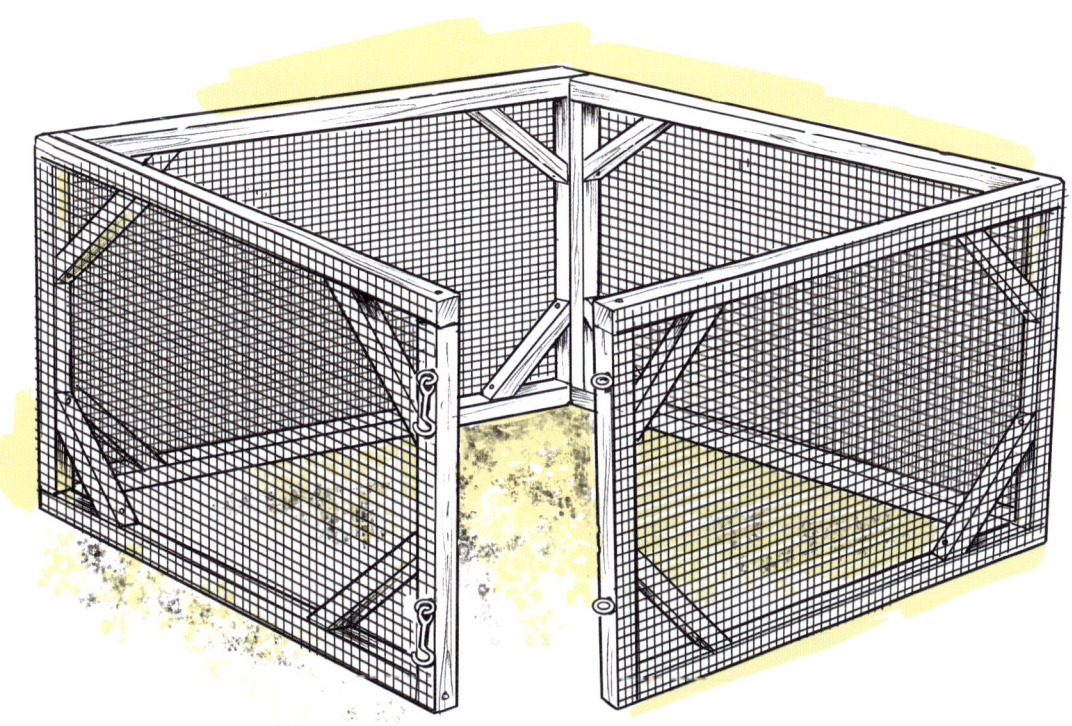

# COMPOST/SOIL SIFTERS

Screening improves the quality of compost, ridding it of worms, debris, and sticks and making it fluffier.

It's a joy to work with screened compost when starting tiny plants or transplanting, or giving houseplants new soil in which to grow. But screening can be a nuisance unless you have the proper equipment.

The sifter shown on a garden cart is ideal for garden use because the screened compost is right there in the cart, ready for transport, as soon as it has found its way through the mesh. Compost is shoveled against the ½-inch wire mesh, and the rejected material falls to the ground, to be shoveled back onto the compost pile.

Serviceable frames can be made from spruce or fir framing lumber, but pressure-treated wood frames will hold up better if you plan to leave the sifters outdoors. And to hold these together firmly, we recommend using waterproof carpenter's glue and galvanized nails.

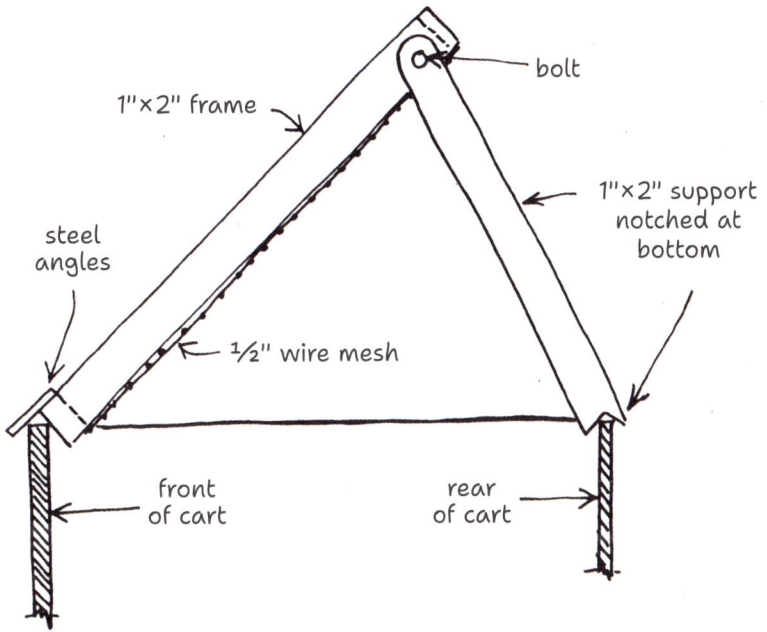

Here is a side view of the sifter cart at left.

## Small Sifters

These small sifters are fine for a small garden, but their use would be tiring if much compost is to be screened.

¼"
wire mesh
nailed to
bottom

4"

8"

8"

¼" or ½"
wire mesh
nailed to
bottom

4"

18"

12"

# PLANT PROTECTORS

Those birds and animals that feast on your just-up seedlings can be discouraged, and there are a few ways to do it.

Cloches are popular in England, where the growing season must be lengthened if some crops are to be harvested. Jam the ends of the arches into the soil and cover with polyethylene or vinyl film. Fold edges of the film around 1×3 strips of wood and staple. You can also make arches of 9- or 12-gauge wire tied with lighter wire at the joints to work in the same way. The frames can be folded for storage.

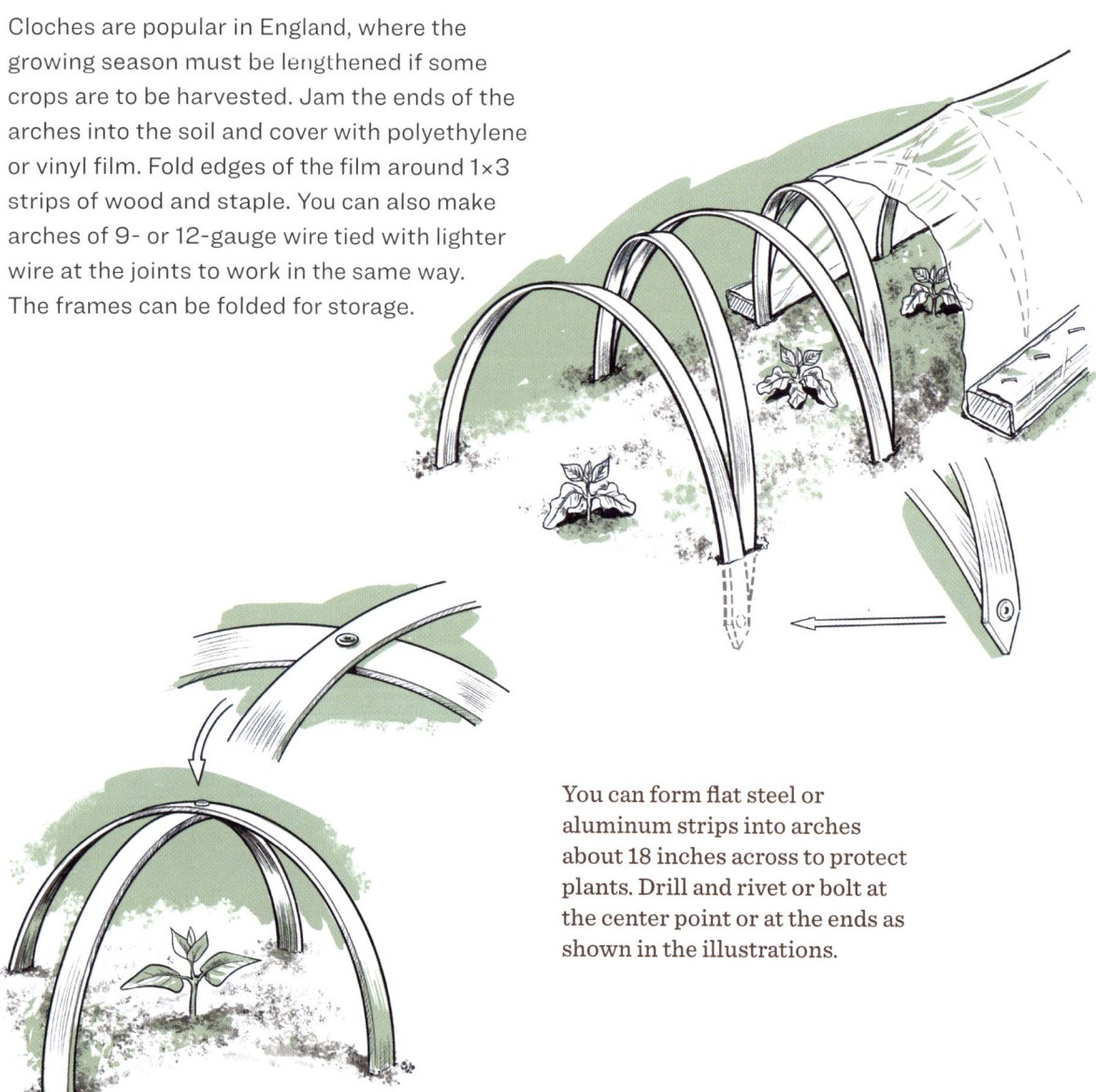

You can form flat steel or aluminum strips into arches about 18 inches across to protect plants. Drill and rivet or bolt at the center point or at the ends as shown in the illustrations.

Or use small-mesh wire fabric to protect young seedlings from being pulled up by birds. Bend wire fabric about 2 inches from edges and bridge planted seed. When the seedlings grow tall enough so the birds can't get them, just remove the mesh wire fabric.

Mesh-reinforced plastic, often used as a substitute for window glass, has a place in the garden. It can be used to protect plants from animals as well as the elements. It is stiff enough to form into arches by stapling the edges to strips of wood. Soil tamped into place will hold the arch in shape.

Cones and cylinders of mesh-reinforced plastic are good for individual plants; arch for tiny plants in a row.

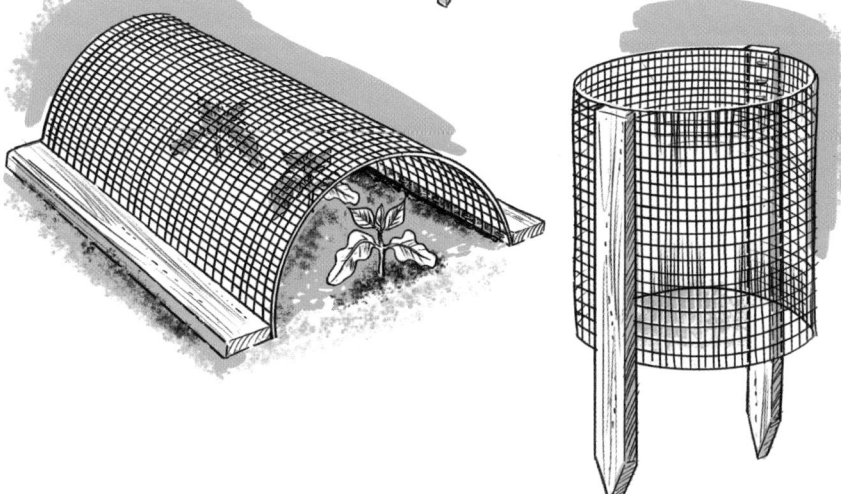

# GARDEN LAYOUT STAKES

Spend 15 minutes now and save hours later. That's the story of garden layout stakes like these.

Once built—and it's a job that can be done in minutes—they will last for years and save you those annual hunts for stakes. Built like those in the illustration, they will ensure that your planting rows are evenly spaced and parallel. Four-foot lengths of any 1×3 wood pieces will do, providing they are sound and fairly straight. The bottom end of the stake should be pointed and measure at least 6 inches from the lower peg to the tip, so it can stand up in soft earth.

The pegs are 6-inch lengths of ½-inch dowel. They should be spaced 3 feet apart on the stakes as shown, so that below the bottom peg there is plenty of room for the stake to be driven into soft earth. Drill all the way through the stakes and glue the pegs in place with waterproof glue. Paint them if you want, and tie enough twine to extend the full width of your garden.

To mark out your rows, just push both stakes into the ground at opposite sides of your first row with the string taut. Once each row is marked out or planted, lay the stakes on their sides and use the dowels to measure the distance to the next row. Then repeat until you get to the other side of the garden bed.

# GARDEN BENCHES

Every garden needs a bench. Among other things, it provides a place to rest your body after hours of work, so that you may contemplate the wonder of gardening: so much from such tiny seeds.

Besides yourself, you can place a dozen other things on a garden bench. Put your trowel on it, and you won't waste time looking for it minutes later. Put your harvest on it—buckets of peas, fat squash, bunches of carrots. Put your sketch pad or journal on it while you tend to some weeds.

The simple garden bench shown below is made from an 8-foot 2×12 (or wider) and is braced with a 2×4. Cut two 14-inch pieces from the plank for legs, leaving a seat area 68 inches long. Center the 2×4 brace between the legs, glue with exterior-type glue, and attach with ¼" × 4" countersunk exterior-grade wood screws. For the sturdiest connection, it's best to drive screws at a slight angle when fastening into the end of a board. Attach legs to top by gluing and using screws. Finish to your own taste.

Or, if you need a lighter bench, make the one on the next page. Want that bench to fold? See the bench on page 81. You'll need three 10-foot 1×4s, one 10-foot ¾" × 2", one 12-foot ½" × 1¼", and one 14-inch 2×2.

# Simple Garden Bench

One of the many virtues of this garden bench (also pictured on the previous page) is that, in addition to its pleasingly simple lines, it takes less than an hour to build but lasts a literal lifetime.

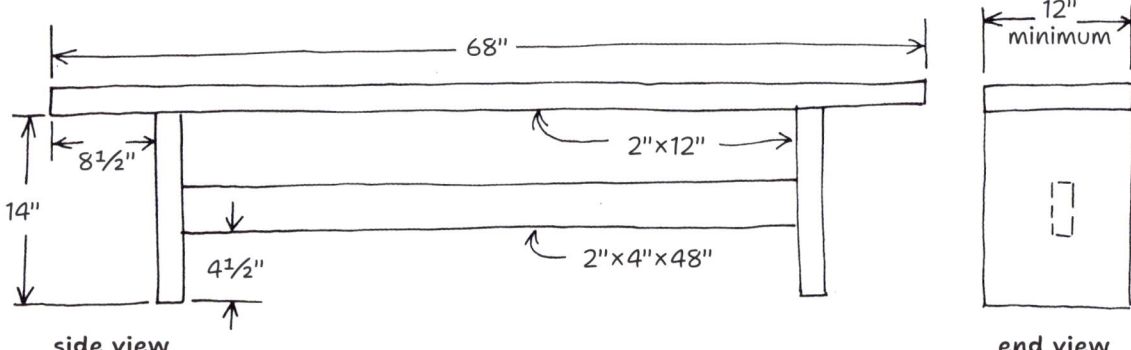

side view                                        end view

# Light Bench

Here's a much lighter bench that will fit well into a smaller garden. Its size and attractive lines make it adaptable to use inside the home as well as outside. Galvanized nails or screws will help this stay sturdy for years.

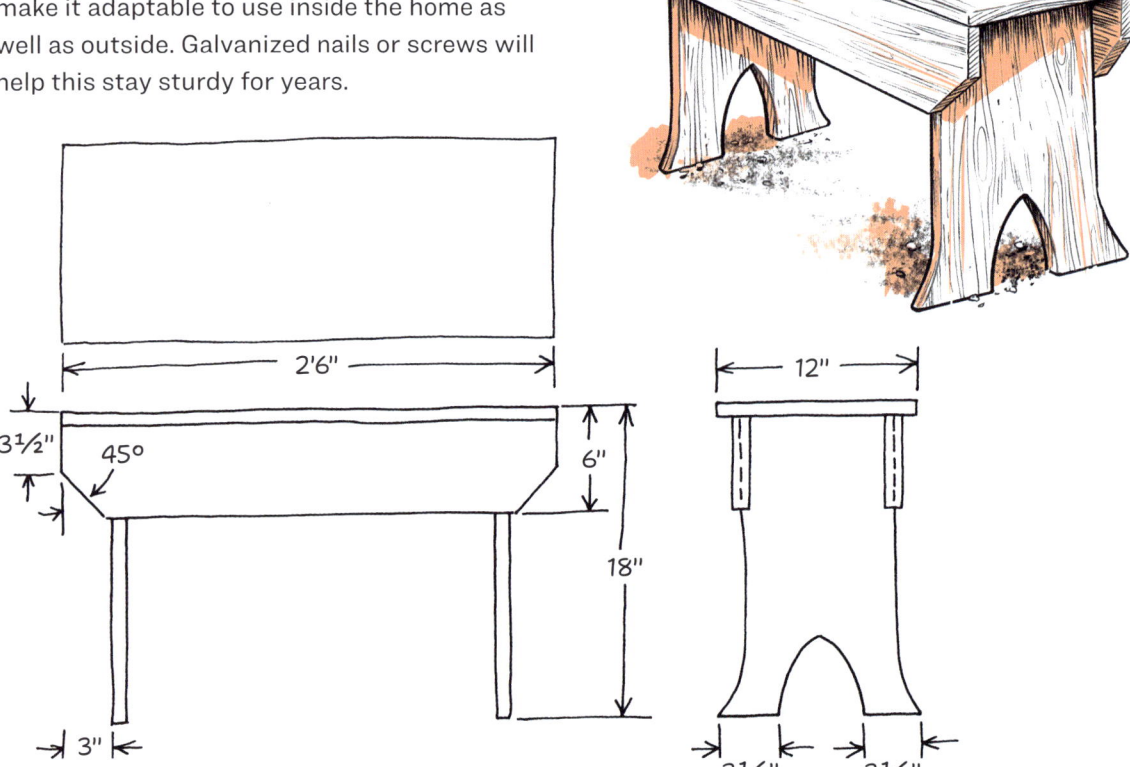

# Folding Bench

If your need is for a light bench that can be moved to various places and is easy to store for the winter, here it is.

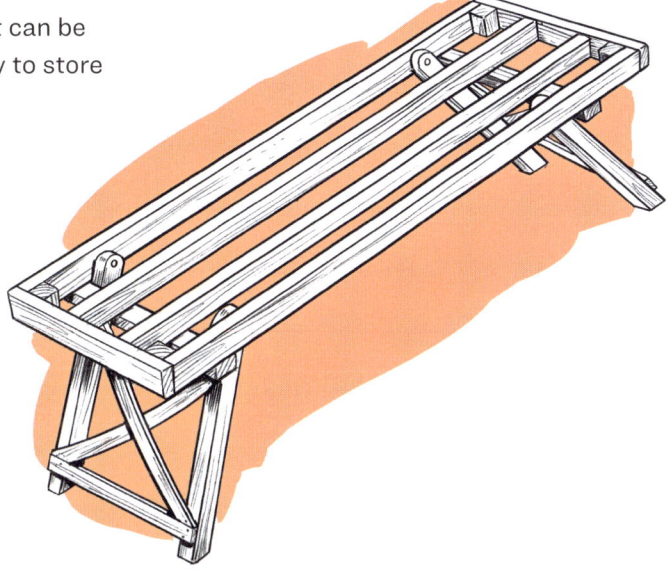

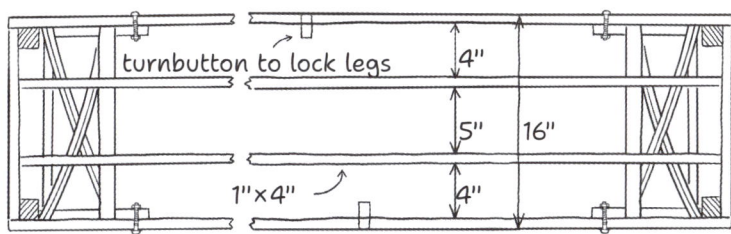

turnbutton to lock legs

4"

5" 16"

1"×4"

4"

**top view**

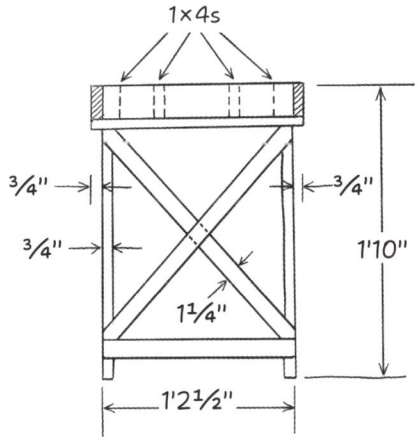

1×4s

3/4"          3/4"

3/4"

1 1/4"

1'10"

1'2 1/2"

**end view**

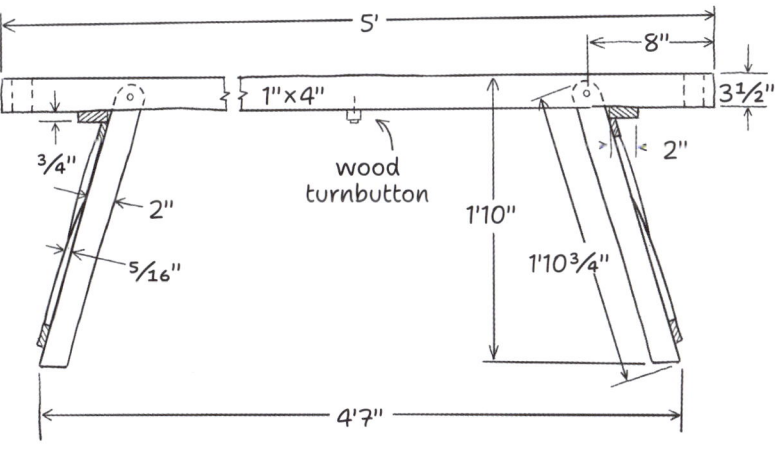

5'

8"

1"×4"

3 1/2"

3/4"

2"

wood turnbutton

1'10"

1'10 3/4"

5/16"

2"

4'7"

**side view**

Handy Box,
page 53

Berry Box,
page 88

Birdhouse,
page 118

Poultry
House,
page 124

Strawberry
Barrel,
page 92

# PICNIC BENCH

There's nothing more pleasant than lunching or dining outdoors in the shade of a tree on a hot summer day. Sit comfortably at this folding picnic table instead of on the ground.

There's nothing more difficult to store for the winter than that big table and bench on which you dined in such comfort in the summer. This bench offers two significant pluses: It's roomy, offering eating space for two adults and at least four young ones. And in the winter it can be folded up and stored out of the way.

To build this you will need two 10-foot 2×4s, two 12-foot 2×4s, one 16-foot 2×4, two 12-foot 1×6s, and one 10-foot 1×6, and two 5-inch T hinges with removable pins. Nail frame temporarily for drilling, use bolts that are ⅜" diameter, and use washers on all bolts.

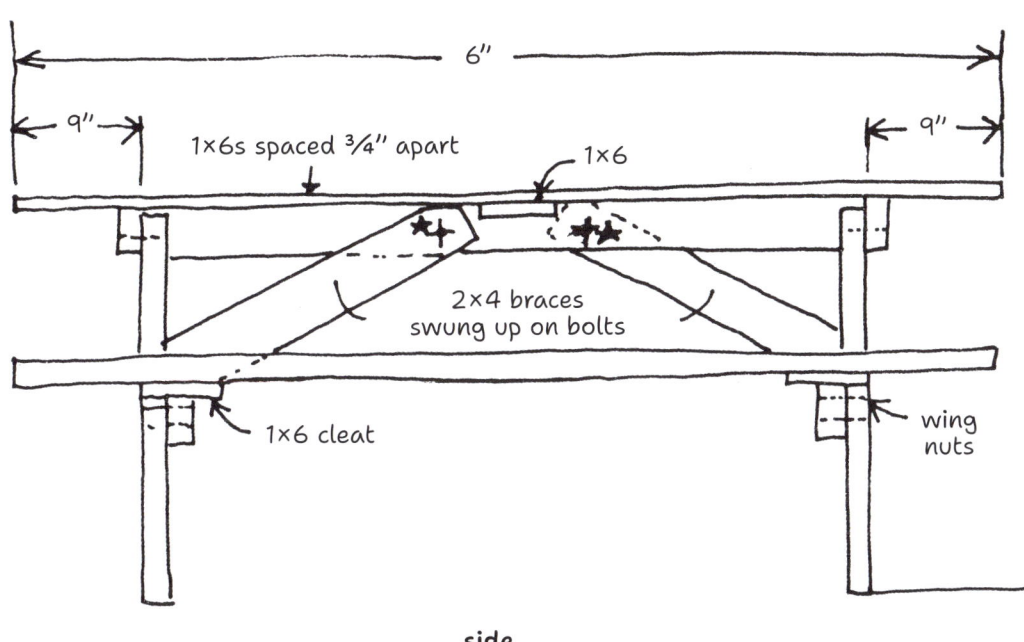

6"

9"

1×6s spaced ¾" apart

1×6

9"

2×4 braces
swung up on bolts

1×6 cleat

wing
nuts

**side**

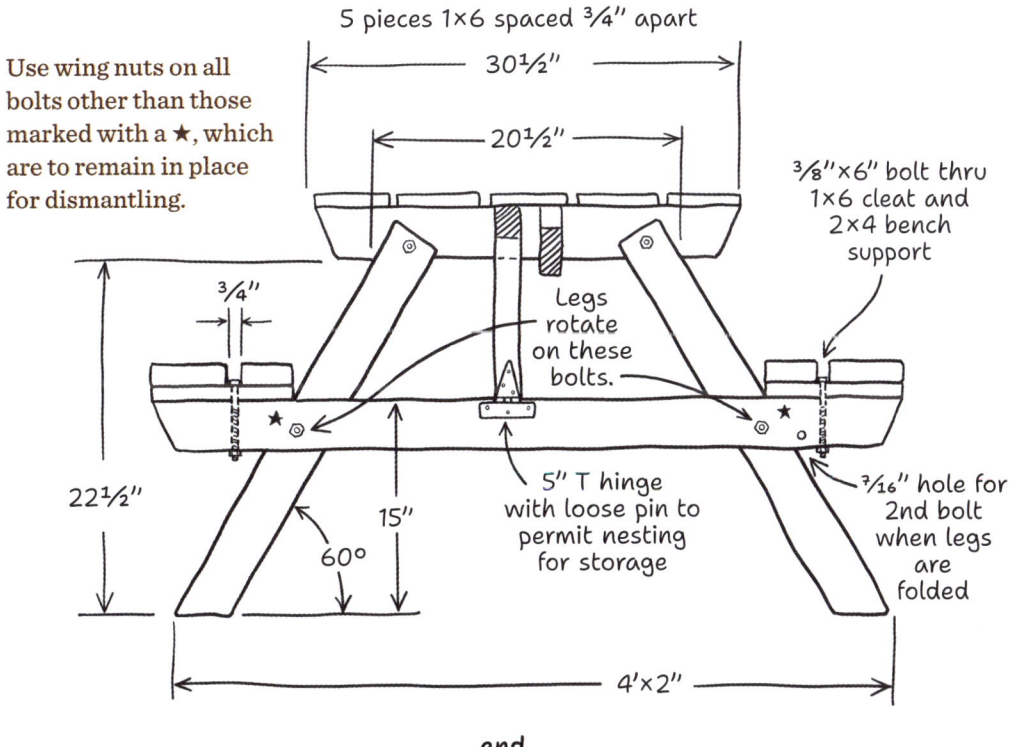

Use wing nuts on all
bolts other than those
marked with a ★, which
are to remain in place
for dismantling.

5 pieces 1×6 spaced ¾" apart

30½"

20½"

⅜"×6" bolt thru
1×6 cleat and
2×4 bench
support

¾"

Legs
rotate
on these
bolts.

22½"

15"

60°

5" T hinge
with loose pin to
permit nesting
for storage

⁷⁄₁₆" hole for
2nd bolt
when legs
are
folded

4'x2"

**end**

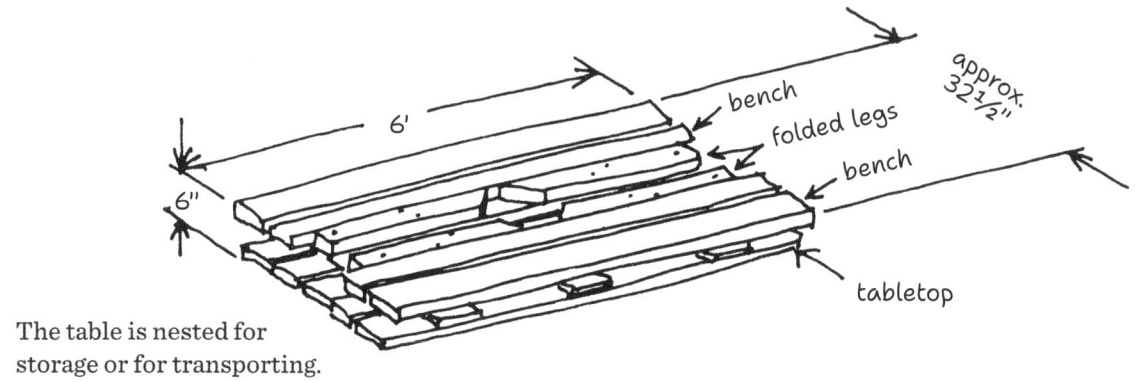

approx. 32½"

6'

6"

bench

folded legs

bench

tabletop

The table is nested for storage or for transporting.

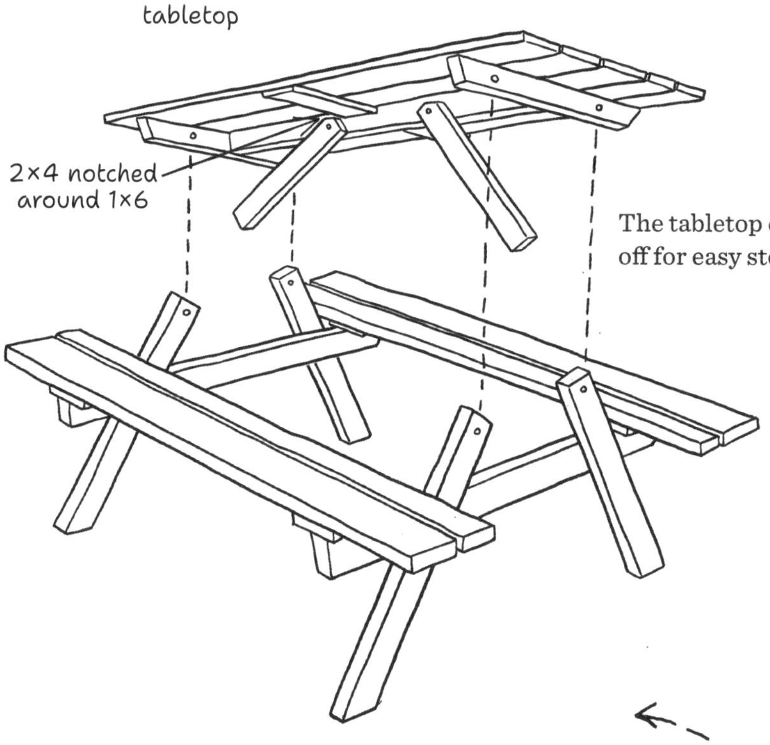

tabletop

2×4 notched around 1×6

The tabletop comes off for easy storage.

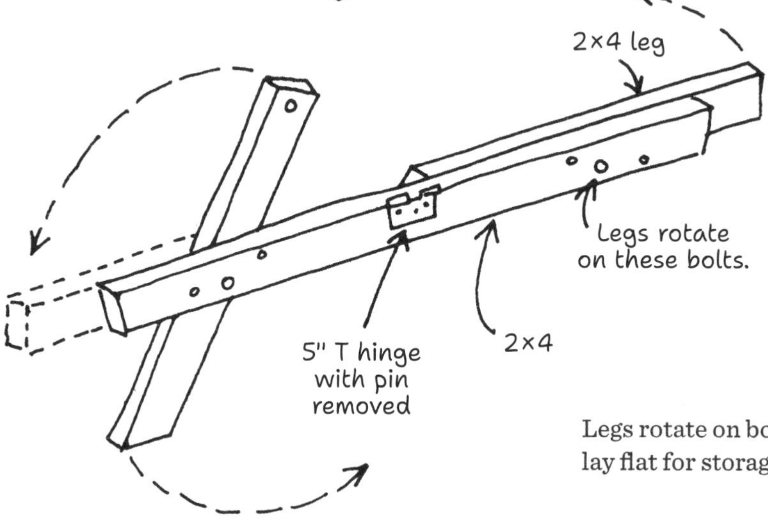

2×4 leg

Legs rotate on these bolts.

5" T hinge with pin removed

2×4

Legs rotate on bolts to lay flat for storage.

# SMOKEHOUSE

If you've picked up a large share of beef or pork from your local CSA farm and you're wondering what you'll do with all that meat, it's time to think about a smokehouse. Here's an easy and inexpensive one to build.

A few simple truths about smoking meat: You need a cool smoke, since you're smoking—not cooking—the meat. You want a constant but not necessarily tremendous amount of smoke to waft past the meat without hanging around. The fuel you select will flavor the meat. Corn cobs are used by some. Hardwoods, not completely dried, are used by many. Softwoods, such as pine and spruce, impart a disagreeable flavor to the meat. And finally, while hams and bacon are the most common meats to smoke, don't be limited to those. Beef, poultry, and fish are delicious after being smoked.

This smokehouse has a smoke chamber made from a metal storage cabinet or file cabinet. Two holes are cut into it: one at the bottom for smoke to enter, and one at the top so smoke will find its way out. The drawing shows a 6-inch terra-cotta tile smoke tunnel, but stovepipe can be substituted. The smoke tunnel is 10 feet long and leads to a fire pit with a metal lid.

# BERRY BOX

Berry pickers, here's a way to prevent crushing those fragile raspberries, and to know exactly how many strawberries you've picked. You'll also find this useful around the garden when picking other small produce.

Make a shallow box, 11″ × 16½″ × 2½″ deep, using light lumber since you'll be carrying it a lot—and full of berries, too, we hope. Attach two 19-inch 1×2s and bring them together at the top, nailing them to a short section of broomstick or a piece of 1×2 for a handle.

Another berrying tip: Leave the caps on your strawberries, as they impart a special sweetness and should not be removed until you are ready to use them. Refrigerate berries for an hour or more, remove cap, and wash in cold water with a few added ice cubes. Drain on paper towels.

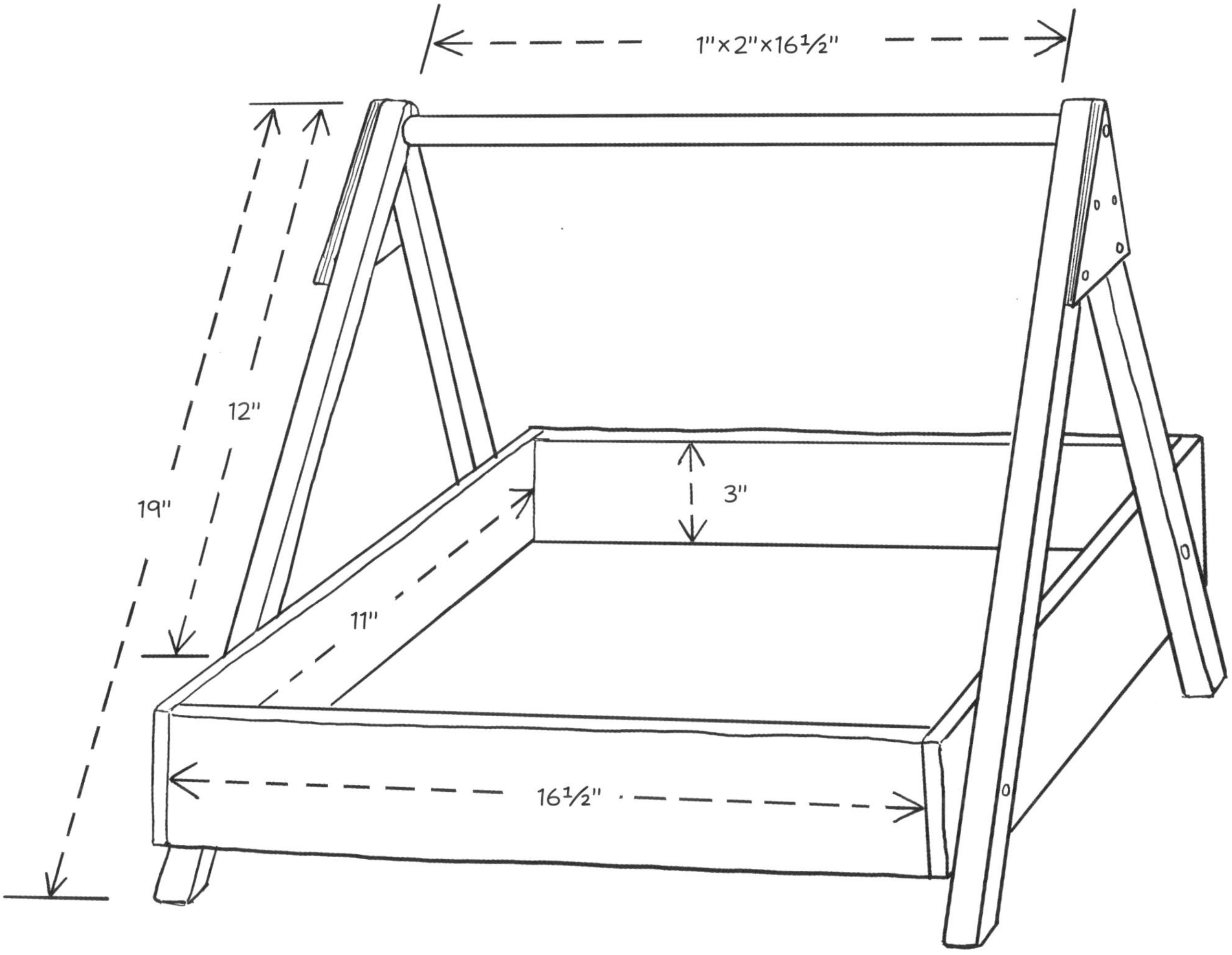

1"×2"×16½"

12"

19"

3"

11"

16½"

This berry box is built to
hold six quart cartons and
can be made from scrap
lumber.

# STRAWBERRY PYRAMID

If you have a spot where you can feature a strawberry pyramid, either of the methods shown here should produce stunning results.

Many people add a fountain effect to their pyramids by installing a sprinkler head in the top center. This, of course, can be fed by a plastic hose buried under the pyramid.

To make the strawberry pyramid pictured below, purchase 38 feet of foot-wide corrugated metal garden edging. This will provide 19 feet for the base circle, 13 feet for the second circle, and 6 feet for the top. Bury the metal strips about 3 inches into the soil. Place the first circle in position and fill it with soil; put the second in position, fill it with soil, then place and fill the third circle. This pyramid will require a surprisingly large amount of topsoil—about 1 cubic yard—but will provide space for 50 strawberry plants.

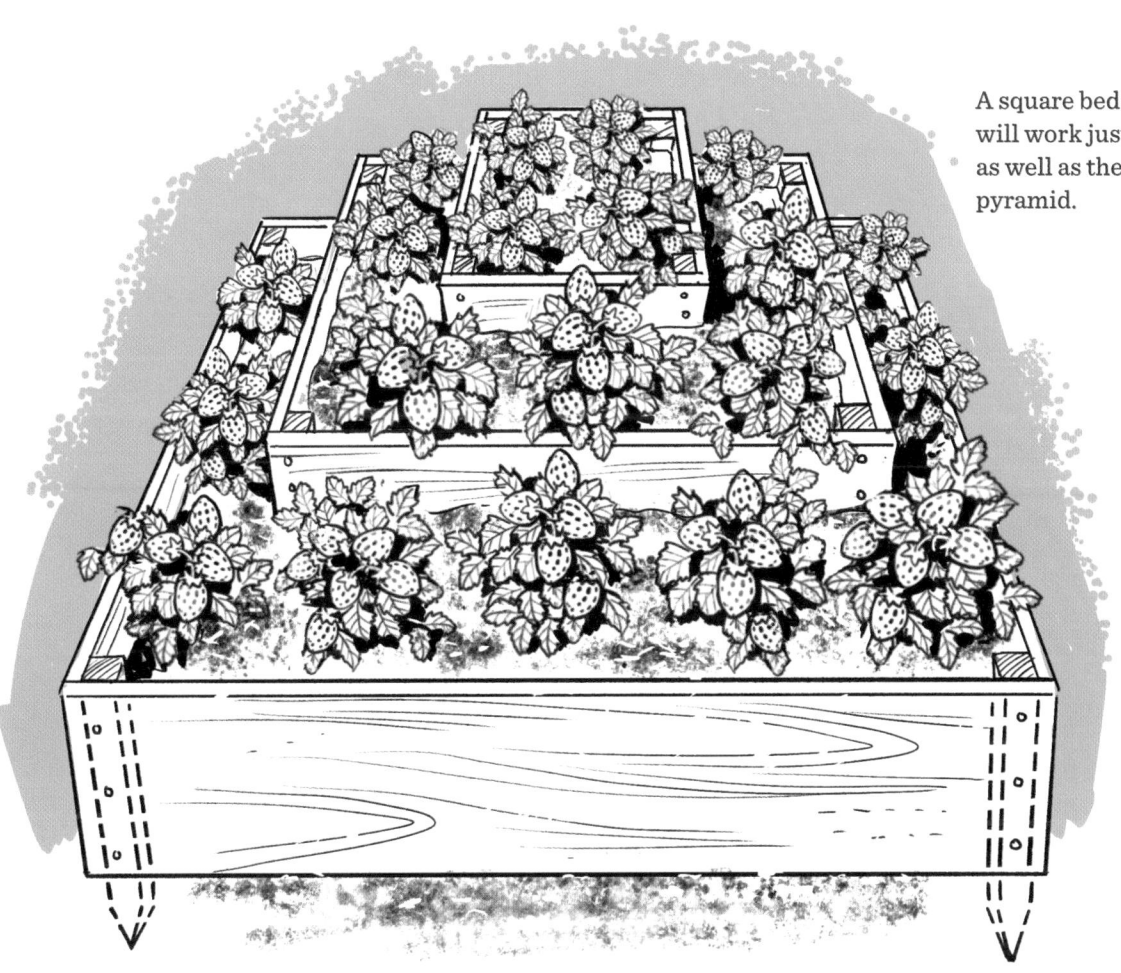

A square bed will work just as well as the pyramid.

Or you can make a square bed of rough-sawn pine or cedar boards, preferably 1×12s. We recommend squares of 60 inches, 36 inches, and 12 inches. If the squares are too large, you will have difficulty working in the beds. Use 24-inch stakes at two corners of each box to hold the squares in position.

By setting out the plants one year, harvesting the next year, and carefully removing old plants after each harvest, letting their space

be filled by the runners that will develop, you can keep this bed in operation for 5 or 6 years. Remember to fight the temptation to crowd the plants. Overly dense foliage will produce smaller berries. Mulching is particularly desirable, since it will conserve moisture, lower the temperatures around the roots, and keep the berries clean. Pine needles will work fine, and their appearance is pleasing.

# STRAWBERRY BARREL

A strawberry barrel provides both beauty and berries. This type of barrel can also be used for sedums and is particularly attractive planted with a variety of smaller herbs, such as basil and creeping thyme.

You'll need a barrel (of course), a rich soil mixture, several shovelfuls of sand, a pail of gravel, a piece of window screening that is 18 inches wide and as long as the barrel is high, several blocks to place under the barrel, and tools to cut the holes. Assemble these where the barrel will be placed. And you will need strawberry plants.

Bore drainage holes in the bottom of the barrel. Then, around the barrel 8 inches from the bottom and 8 inches apart, cut holes for the plants. An easy way to cut these is to bore a triangle of holes 2 inches apart, then cut between them with a coping saw. Stagger similar rows of holes up the side of the barrel, with holes never closer than 8 inches.

Put 3 to 4 inches of gravel or small stones in the bottom of the barrel for drainage. Roll window screening into a long tube about 5 inches in diameter and tie it in with wire. Place the tube in the center of the barrel where, when it is filled with sand, it will serve as a conduit to get water to the soil at all levels.

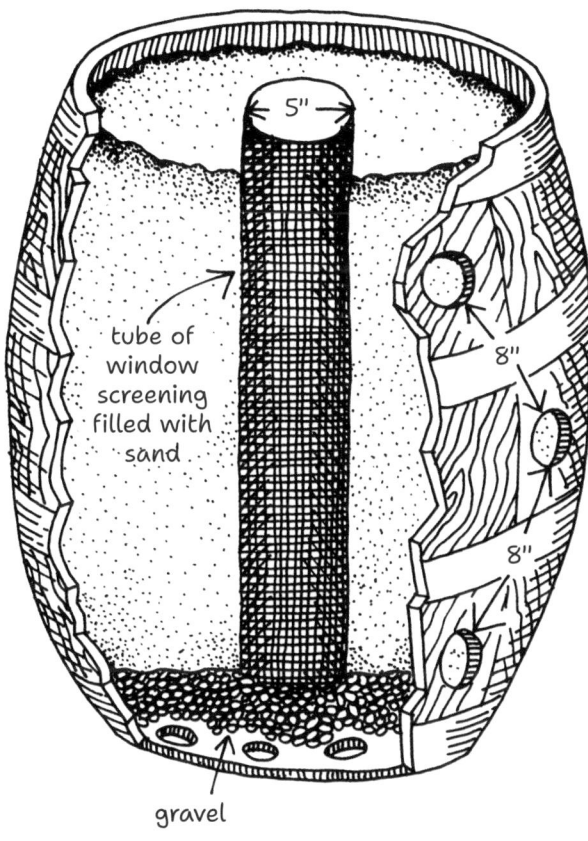

The tube of window screen in the center of the barrel will funnel water to plants at every level.

Begin putting soil mixture (half potting mix and half compost) into the barrel, and sand into the tube, until both reach halfway up the first row of triangles. Plant each strawberry plant along the side of the barrel, with the crown of plant and foliage protruding out of each hole. Water the barrel, making certain the crowns and plants don't settle below the level of the holes in the barrel. Fill the barrel to the next level of holes and repeat the process. When the barrel is filled, plant a few plants 8 inches apart on top.

Shift the barrel a quarter-turn counterclockwise every few days to balance light on the plants. Like all strawberry plants, these should not be allowed to produce fruit the first year. Keep blossoms picked so that growth will go into plants. Don't let plants produce runners, either, unless a few are needed to replace dead plants in the barrel.

After the first heavy frost, move the barrel into the garage or barn, or wrap it in a blanket of straw or hay, to protect plants.

# MASSIVE POTS

If you need massive pots for outdoor planting and the prices of store-bought ones are discouraging, visit your home construction store and check their selection of terra-cotta tiles.

Set in place, and with a small piece of plastic underneath to prevent plant roots from extending into the soil, these flue tiles make dramatic plant holders. A drawback is that they may be more difficult to move than conventional pots, since soil will drop out of the bottom unless they are handled very carefully. A strong point is that they have excellent drainage. No plants will drown in them, as in pots without holes in their bottoms.

# PLANT SUPPORTS

Most plants benefit from being supported. Positive outcomes include fewer diseases, additional garden space if plants are trained to grow upright, and room to mulch.

When tomatoes, squash, and other fleshy vegetables are kept off the ground, they are less likely to develop mold and rot caused by dampness or fungus in the earth. With the stalks and leaves off the ground, you can easily apply mulch around the base of the plant. By training plants to grow upright, you will conserve considerable space, and with land becoming scarcer and gardens by necessity having to be smaller, you can grow more on a smaller piece of land.

Many gardeners contend that you can raise more tomatoes if you don't tie them up in any way and just let them run along the ground. And we agree. You will have more tomatoes—more for the slugs. More to rot. More to step on as you reach for a faraway tomato.

For the best crop, get those vines off the ground.

There are many ways to do it. The most-used system is a stake pounded deep into the ground for good support and the tomato plant tied to it with material that will not cut into the plant. Strips torn from old sheets work fine. For many plants, 6 feet of stake above ground is not too much.

Try several of the following methods for holding tomato plants off the soil. You will soon know which method yields the highest number of tomatoes with the least amount of work.

95

# Tomato Cylinder

Of the many methods of holding tomatoes upright, we vote for the tomato cylinder. Concrete reinforcing wire with a 6-inch mesh and 5 feet in width is ideal. Cut a 4-foot piece, round it into a cylinder, and tie it in shape with wire. Set it over the tomato plant, and hold it there with two stakes. It's easy to train the vines in this cylinder, and picking tomatoes is a joy, particularly if you have struggled with sprawling, earthbound vines before.

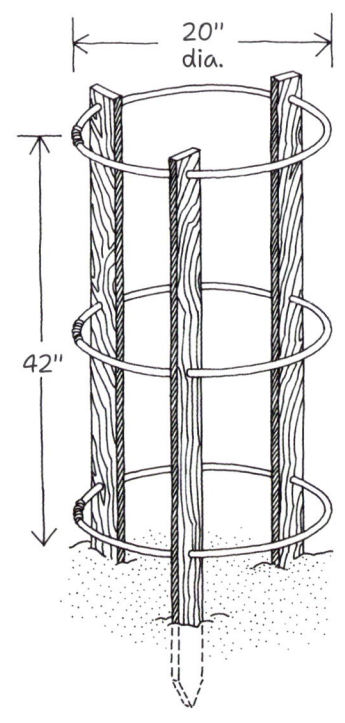

# Triangle Supports

Make triangle supports using 9- or 12-gauge wire. Triangles should be 20 inches on each side. Clamp three pieces of lath together and drill three ½–inch holes as shown. Slip the triangles through holes and bind ends together with lighter wire. Make sure the triangles are the same size, otherwise they will not fold neatly.

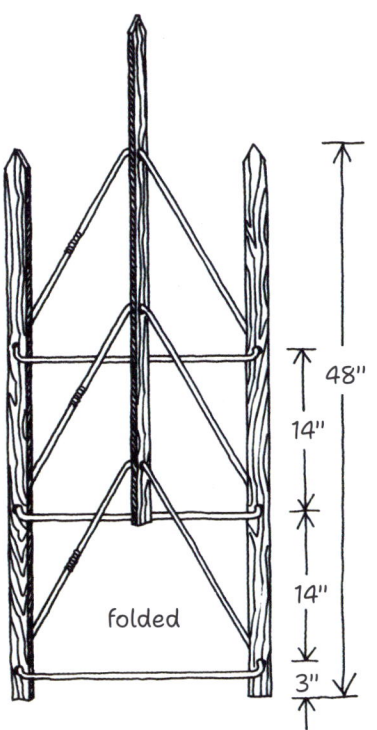

# Tomato Frame

Here is a compromise arrangement for tomatoes that keeps them off the ground yet lets them grow in their natural horizontal position. This was designed using 1″ × 2″ frames and 1×2 mesh wire. The 3′ × 6′ frame is held 8 inches off the ground by stakes or concrete blocks. The tomatoes are planted under the frame and fed up through the mesh when still young.

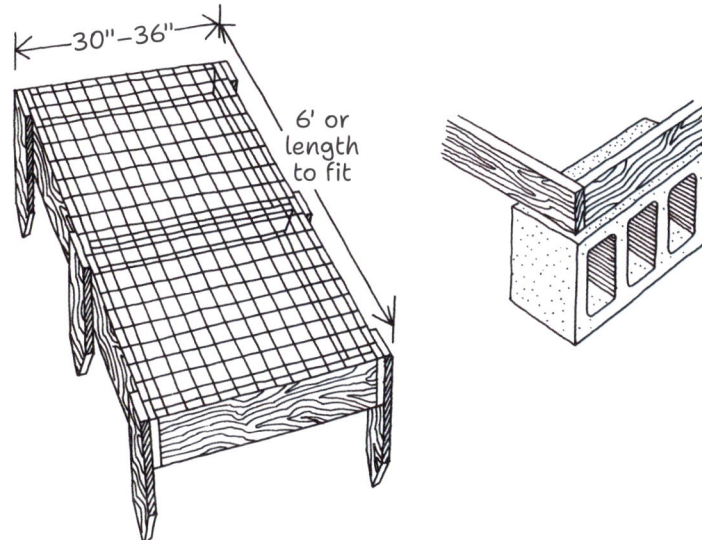

# Pole Supports

The support shown here involves poles with heavy cord at 6-inch intervals so, as it grows, you can weave the tomato plant through the cords. Remember, there will be a lot of weight on those big plants, so don't plan for more than two plants between each set of poles.

A similar method to the pole and cord support for tomatoes shown above is to nail or tie thin poles (saplings are fine) between the poles and then tie the tomato plants to them.

# GARDEN FENCES

A fence around a garden, complete with a gate, adds a note of neatness to your spread. And it serves practical purposes, too.

Cucumbers, peas, and other vegetables will grow on it, and it will halt dogs, roving children, and whatever wild animals want a helping of your produce. Putting up a fence is a lot of work, but the extra effort will pay off in the years ahead as the fence stands straight and solid.

If it's to be mostly decorative, you have your choice of many materials, from split rails to metal. If it's woodchucks, rabbits, or other tunneling pests you're trying to keep out, pick 5-foot chicken wire and bury the bottom 1 foot down, with a foot bent toward the outside to make an underground L shape, for those critters who try digging underneath. If it's squirrels, use two strands of electric fencing—one near the outer side and a few inches from the ground, the other 1 to 2 inches above the top. If you're trying to stop raccoons, forget it. They'll find their way into the First National Bank vault if there's sweet corn locked in there.

Before building that gate, think about location and use. See page 104 for particulars.

Remember those wild visitors. If you have animal problems, make certain the gate is tight, without squeezing-through room on the sides or the bottom. At the bottom, it may be necessary to have the gate swing out of the garden and, when closed, butt against a low rock step.

## Setting Posts

When building a fence, as with many other structures, it's necessary to set posts in the ground. If you use wooden posts, try for cedar ones, which last for quite some time in the ground. Pressure-treated posts will last longer, and you can get special plastic post sleeves to keep them from contacting the soil if you're concerned about the chemical preservatives being near your veggies. Steel posts are cheap and simple to install for wire fences, too. Get the posts fence-high plus 2 feet so they can be deep and firm in the ground. A 10-foot span between fence posts is a good average. Pick solid posts for the corners and anchor them well. Do the same for the posts that will support the gate.

Set posts 2 feet deep for a 5-foot-high fence, 2½ feet for a 6-foot fence, and 3 feet for most 8- to 10-foot structures. Wood fence posts will last longer if the tops are cut at an angle to shed water.

# Five Ways to Set Posts

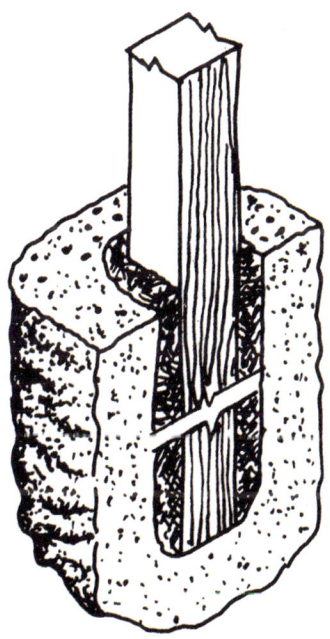

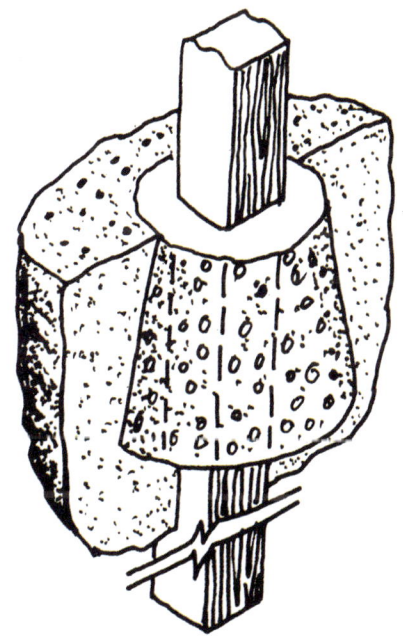

**1. Gravel and earth.** The simplest method of setting a post is to dig a hole, set the post in the ground, then tamp earth around it. Better yet, fill the hole around the post with gravel or crushed stone, tamp it, and you will have a stable and well-drained post.

**2. Concrete collar.** If the soil is sandy or unstable, pour a concrete collar around the post after it has been set in the hole and earth tamped around it. You may need a temporary brace to hold the post while the concrete sets.

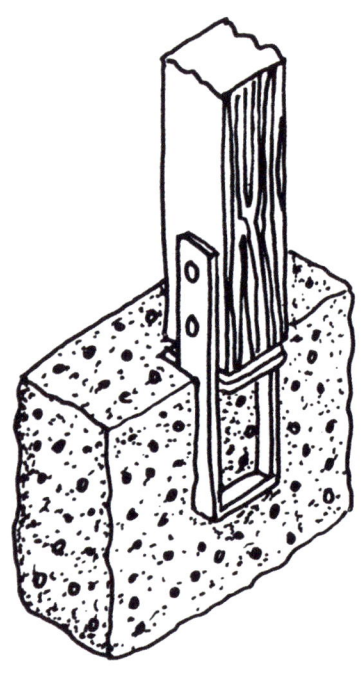

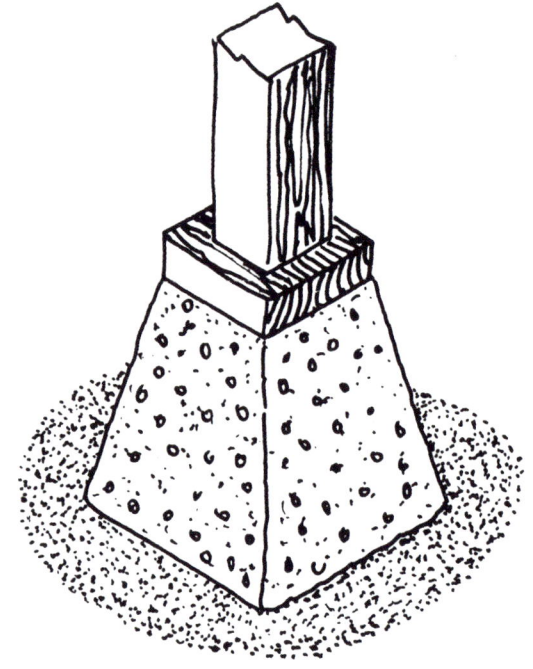

**3. Post anchors.** When putting posts in concrete, you can use post anchors, available at building supply dealers.

**4. Block in concrete.** Another method is to embed a block into the concrete, then nail the post to that. This is less secure than the post anchor.

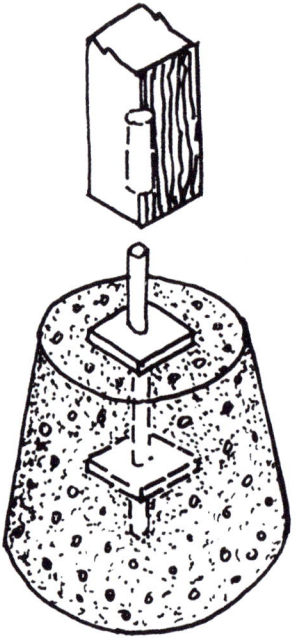

**5. Drift pin.** When you want a concealed anchorage, you can use a drift pin. Leave a small space between the bottom of the post and the concrete surface to avoid the accumulation of moisture and dirt.

## Setting Corner Posts

The corner posts receive the greatest punishment, and they are usually the first to fail. Build them strong, brace them well, and they'll stand the test of the years.

Here are three methods of building a strong corner assembly.

**Single bracing.** Two 8-foot posts span the distance between the corner post and the other two. The corner unit is pulled tightly together by double strands of 9-gauge wire, extending from the tops of the two posts to the bottom of the corner post. This wire can be tightened, as shown, by twisting it with a stick.

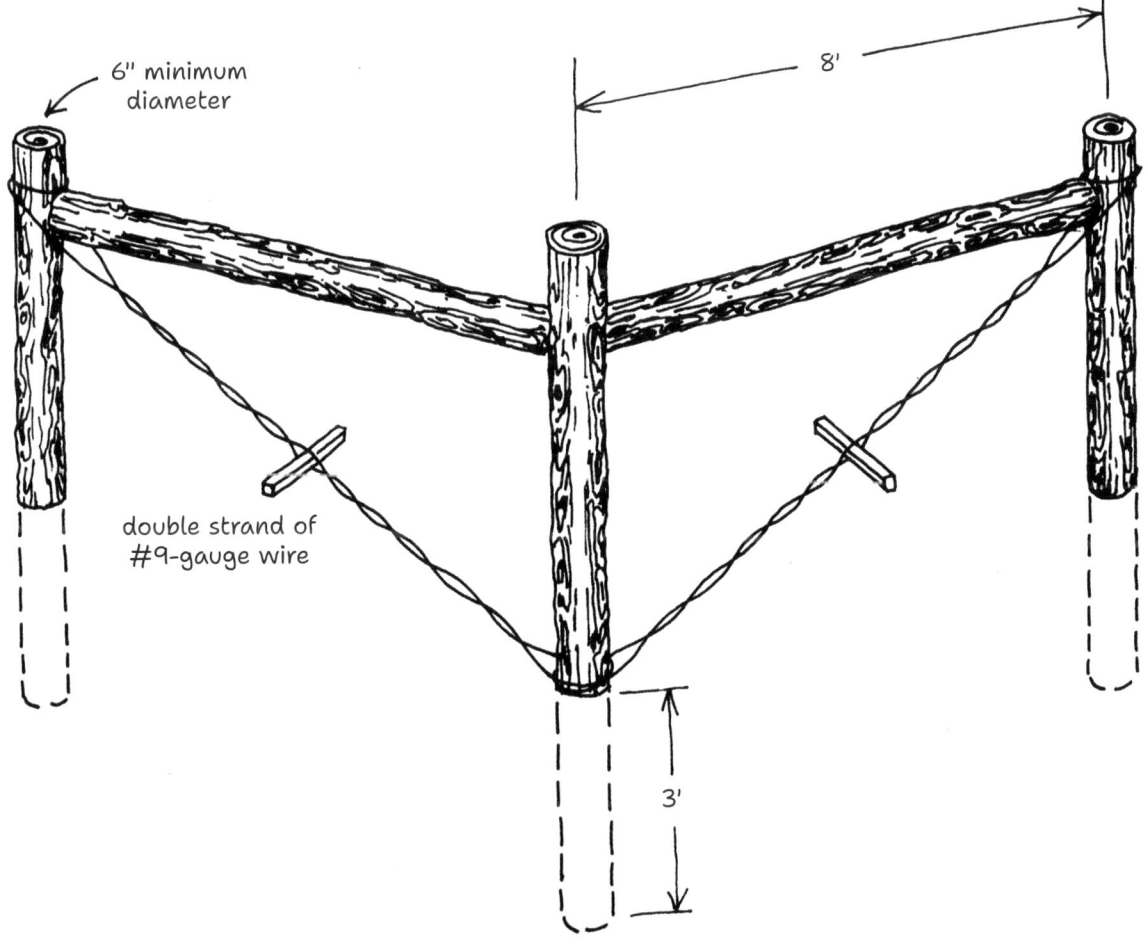

6" minimum diameter

8'

double strand of
#9-gauge wire

3'

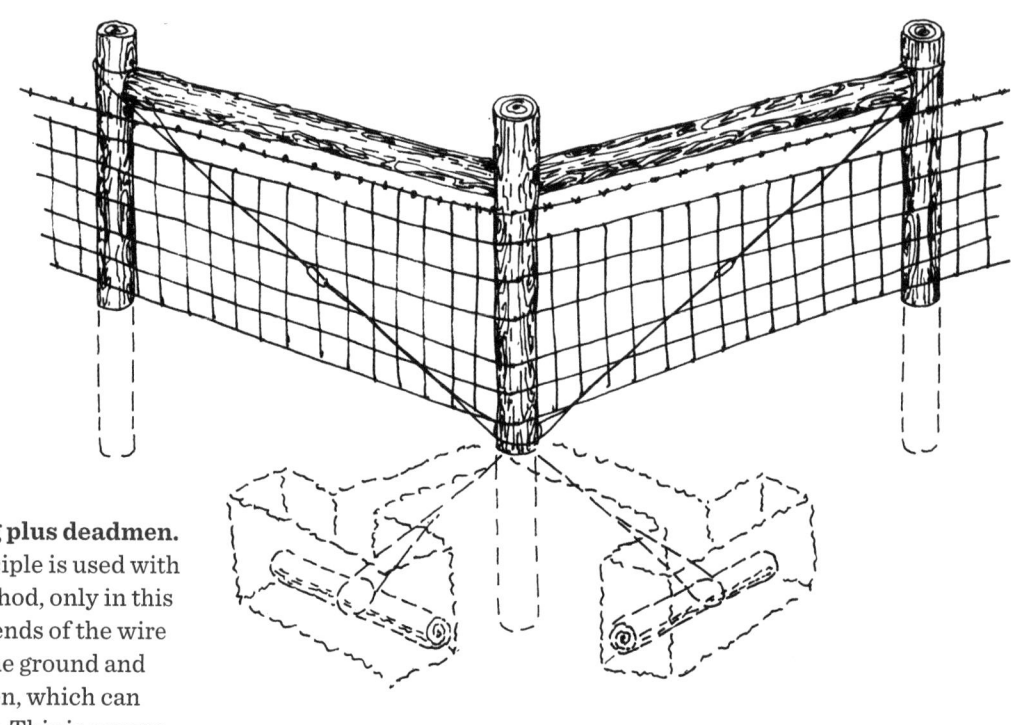

**Single bracing plus deadmen.** The same principle is used with the second method, only in this case the lower ends of the wire are sunk into the ground and held by deadmen, which can be rocks or logs. This is a more permanent arrangement.

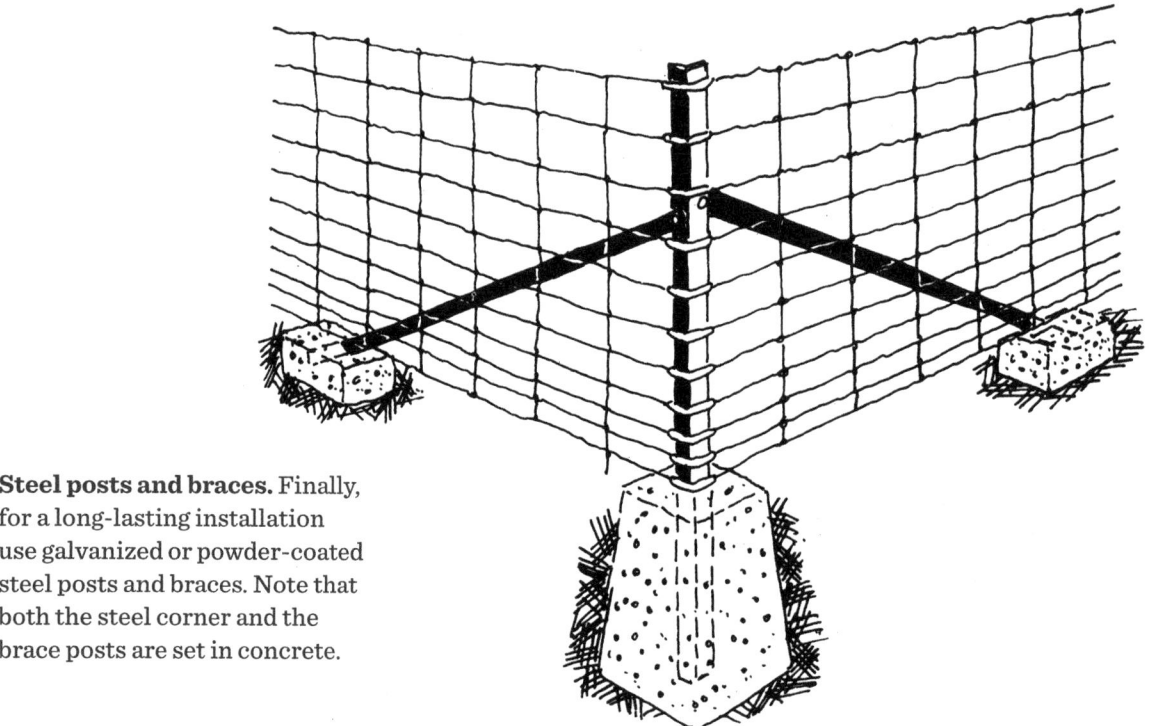

**Steel posts and braces.** Finally, for a long-lasting installation use galvanized or powder-coated steel posts and braces. Note that both the steel corner and the brace posts are set in concrete.

## Tightening Fence

The graceful lines of loose fencing are not appreciated by fence builders, nor do they strengthen or increase the efficiency of the fence.

The trick is: How to get the fence tight? Try one of these methods.

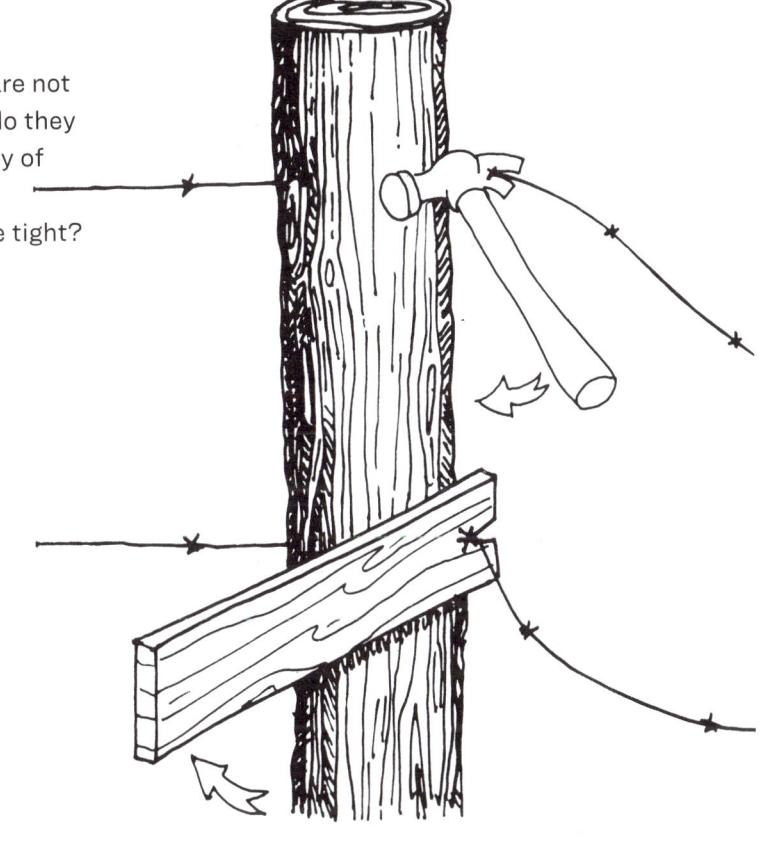

**For barbed wire,** use a claw hammer or a notched hardwood board to hold the wire while you staple it into place. Drive the staples at an angle to the wood's grain to avoid splitting.

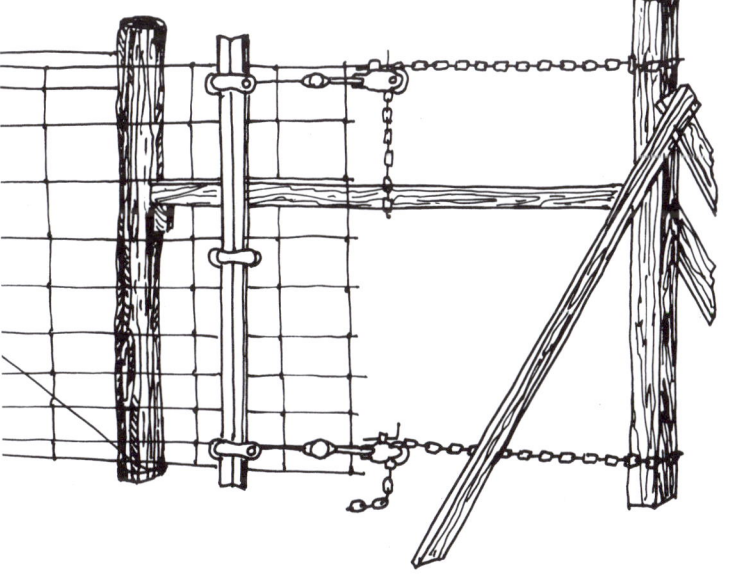

**For a woven fence,** use a fence stretcher such as this. Note the braced "dummy" post at right.

# GATES

You'll want to plan before deciding on the gate you want for your fence. It should fit in with the style of your fence and your garden.

And the location for the gate is important. It should be accessible from the path between house and garden. Don't have it open into the strawberry patch or the asparagus bed, for example; it should open onto a path that brings you into the rest of the garden. A poor location can be an irritating nuisance.

No matter what style you choose, your gate should be:

- **Wide enough** for you and any equipment to get into the garden. Three feet wide is a minimum. Measure the widest cart or tiller you will be taking into the garden, and allow a minimum of 6 inches leeway.

- **Sturdy** because a child will swing on it and test it. You will bump into it with your garden cart. Adults will lean on it.

- **Braced,** so that it will not sag. The diagonal brace is usually a must.

- **Hung on sturdy poles.** Anchor them well: 4×4 posts set several feet into the ground surrounded by compacted gravel will support an average-size gate, but if you plan to build a heavy or long gate, consider increasing the posts to 6×6 and setting them in concrete.

- **Equipped with rustproof hardware.** Rusted hardware will fail, compromising your fence.

- **Constructed low enough** so that the space between it and the ground does not permit entrance of the very animals you are trying to exclude.

- **Built to open downhill** if your garden is on a slope. Otherwise it will bump into the uphill surface of your garden path.

Here's an important construction law to obey when building a gate: A rectangle with its four sides is unstable, but a triangle is firm. Without those diagonals, this gate would have a tendency to sag at the top, making it difficult to open and shut. A gate with some such imperfection can become a constant source of irritation.

With a light gate you may get the same stiffness using a wire diagonal tightened with a turnbuckle, such as you may have on your screen door.

# Simple Gate

Here is a simple gate that illustrates some of the points mentioned on page 104. Note the framework is built of 2×4s to give it strength. The posts are sturdy and held in place with concrete.

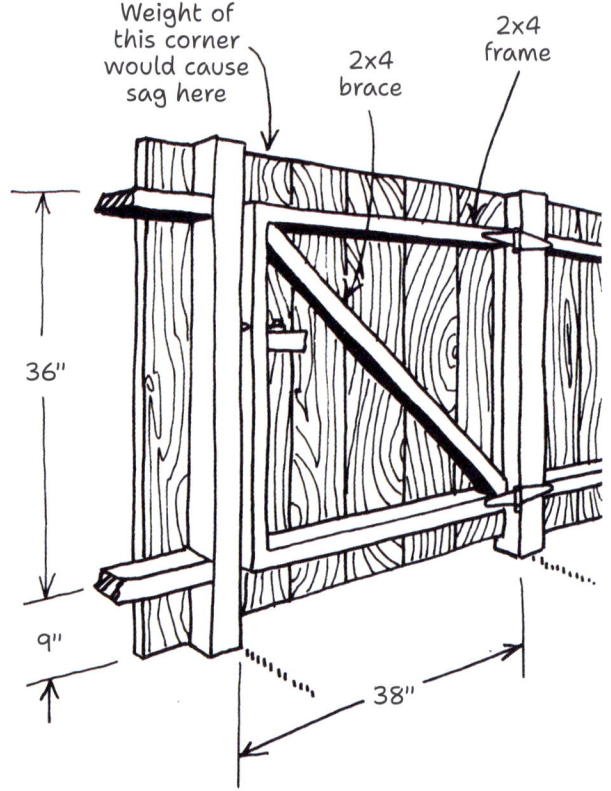

Weight of this corner would cause sag here

2x4 brace

2x4 frame

36"

9"

38"

# Foot-Operated Gate

If you often approach a gate with arms loaded, the gate at right is the one for you. Note that it is foot-operated on one side and hand-operated on the other. Consider this when you install the gate. And, while these drawings do not show it, a diagonal brace is needed to prevent this from sagging.

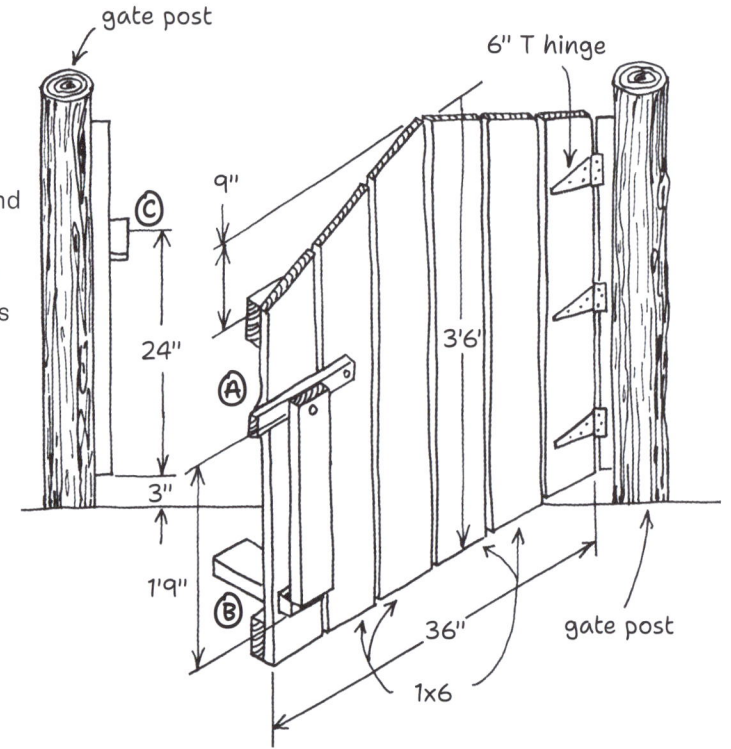

gate post

6" T hinge

9"

Ⓒ

24"

Ⓐ

3'6'

3"

1'9"

Ⓑ

36"

1x6

gate post

## foot-operated gate details

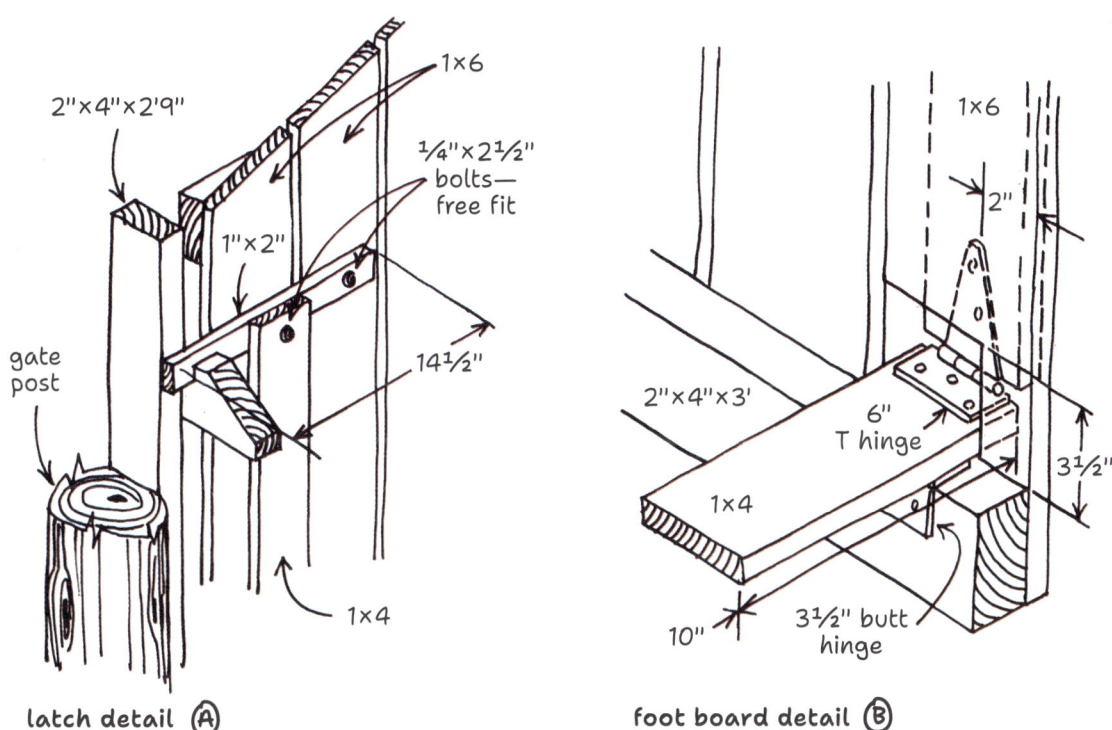

2"×4"×2'9"

1×6

¼"×2½" bolts— free fit

1"×2"

gate post

14½"

1×4

**latch detail Ⓐ**

1×6

2"

2"×4"×3'

6" T hinge

1×4

3½"

10"

3½" butt hinge

**foot board detail Ⓑ**

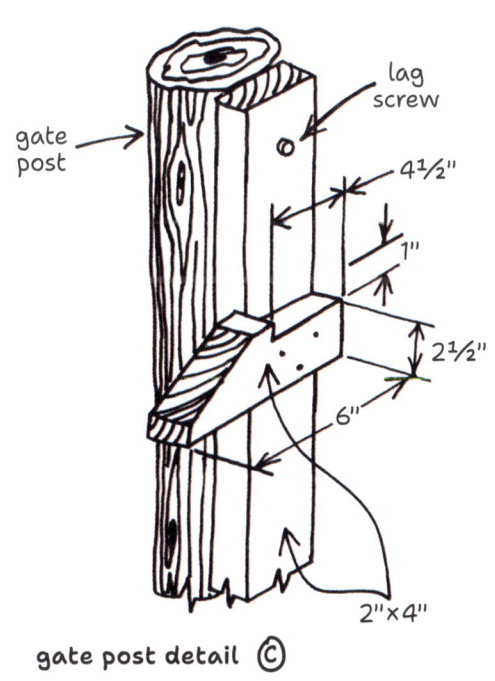

gate post

lag screw

4½"

1"

2½"

6"

2"×4"

**gate post detail Ⓒ**

# Stone Fence Gate

If your ambition was so great that you created a stone wall, you have a slight problem in attaching a gate to it. The stone fence gate below is a relatively simple method, which involves anchoring pressure-treated 2×6s (or other rot-resistant wood) on both ends of the stone wall. This can be done, as shown, by running long screw eye bolts through the planks and cementing them into the wall, shimming or clamping them as needed to hold them plumb and square to the gate opening until the cement sets. Then hang the gate as if those anchored planks were the fence posts.

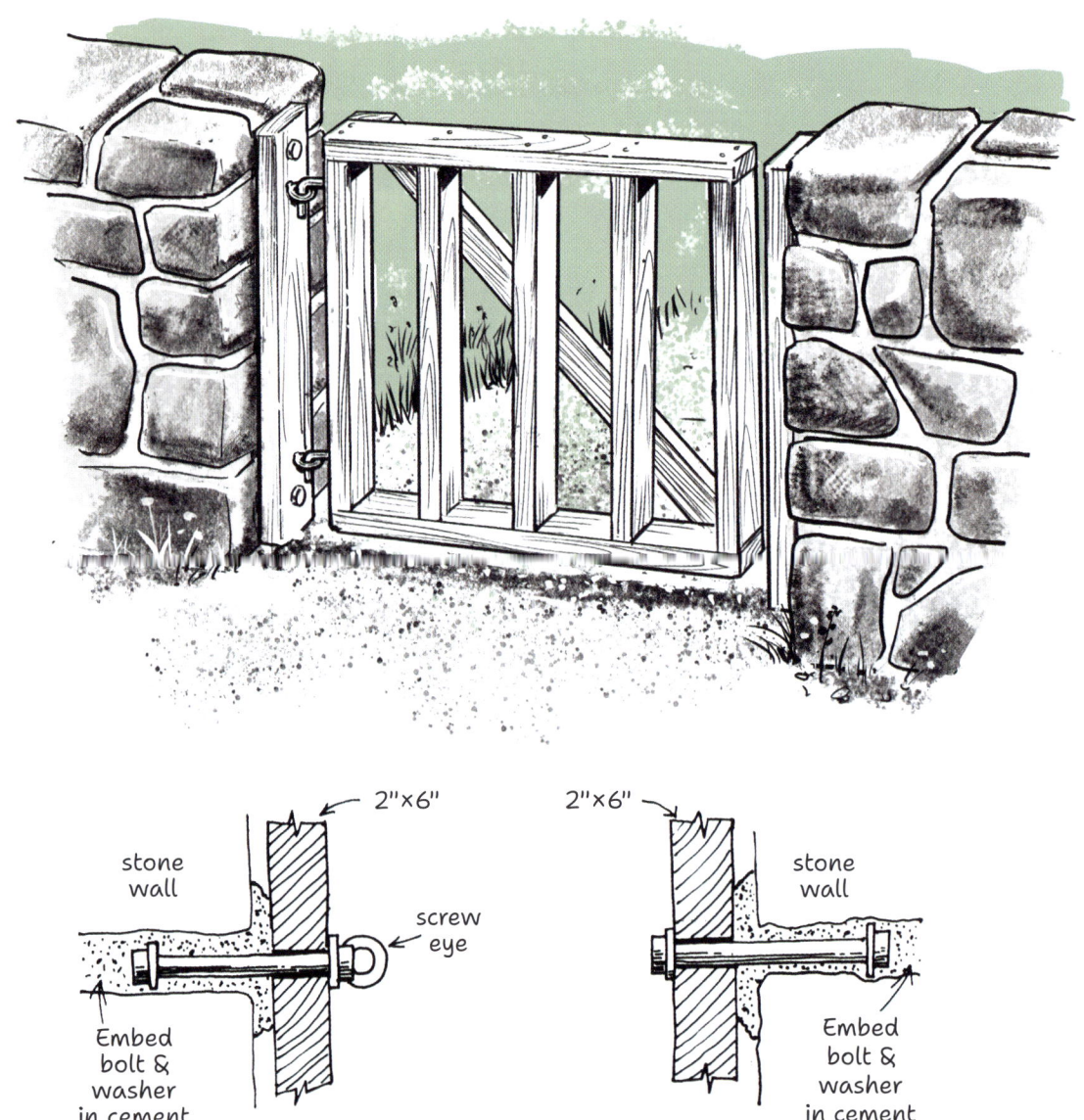

2"×6"

stone wall

screw eye

Embed bolt & washer in cement

2"×6"

stone wall

Embed bolt & washer in cement

# Gate Hinge

This is where the true test of your gate takes place, right at the hinge. Is it strong enough to bear the weight of the gate? Does it bind in some disconcerting fashion? Does it squeak (something you might like or hate)?

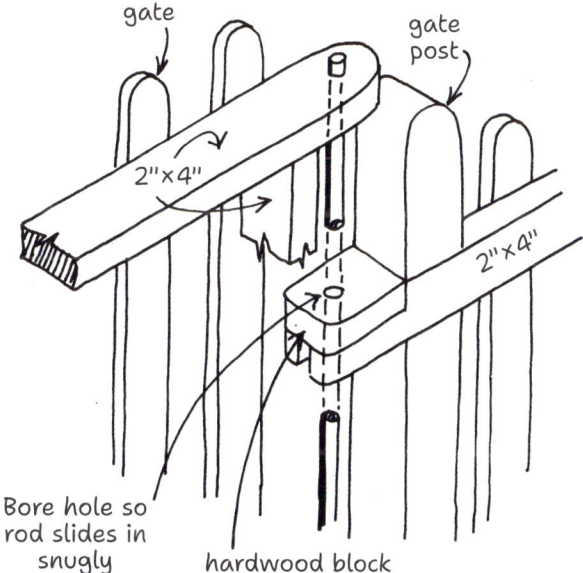

gate

gate post

2"×4"

2"×4"

Bore hole so rod slides in snugly

hardwood block

Here's a simple way to hang a comparatively light gate, with a galvanized or stainless steel rod that pierces both the gate and fence crosspieces where they overlap.

see detail above

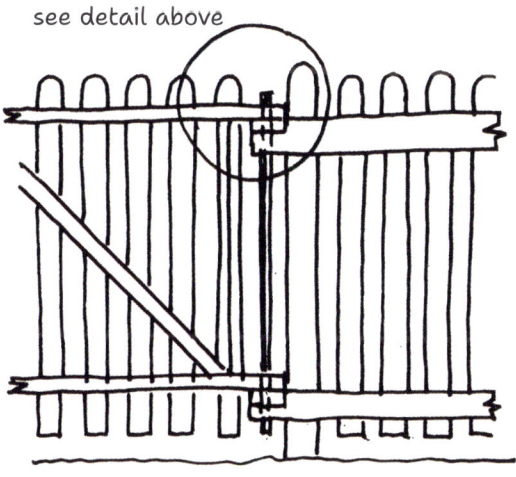

# Gate Latches

You can purchase gate latches at your hardware store, but it's easy to build a latch that will be far more decorative. Here are a few simple ones that can be made of wood.

**gravity latch**

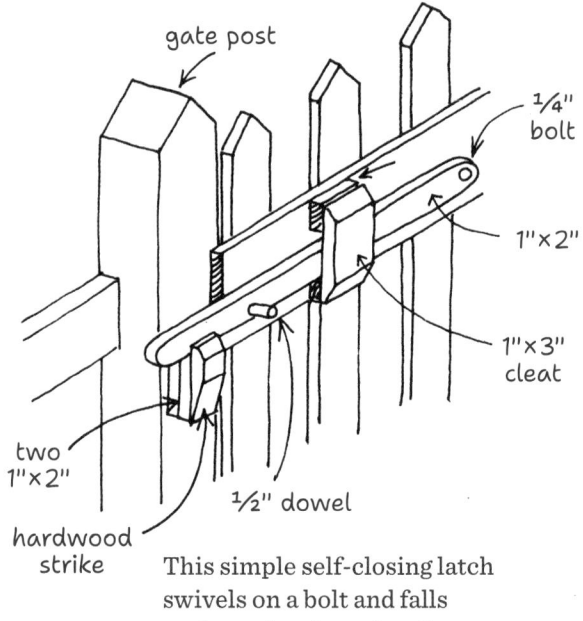

gate post

¼" bolt

1"×2"

1"×3" cleat

two 1"×2"

hardwood strike

½" dowel

This simple self-closing latch swivels on a bolt and falls against a hardwood strike.

**sliding latch**

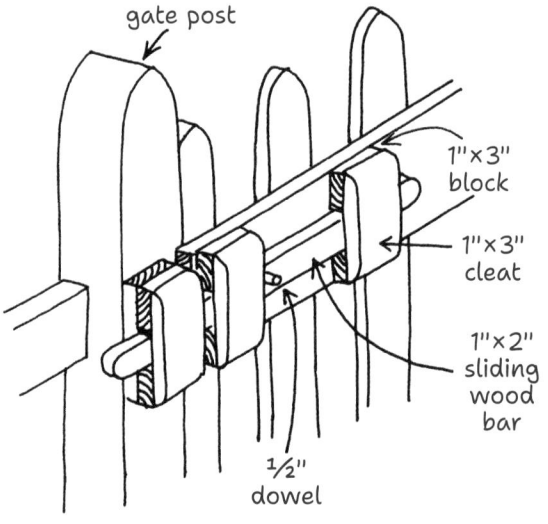

gate post

1"×3" block

1"×3" cleat

1"×2" sliding wood bar

½" dowel

A ½" dowel enables you to slide the latch open and closed.

drop latch

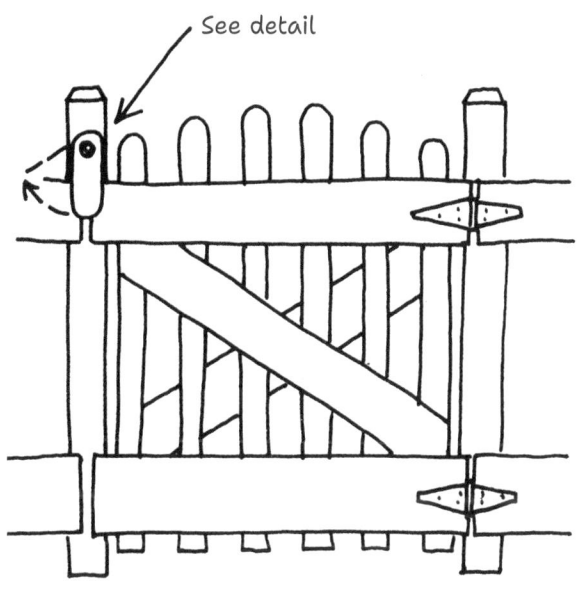

See detail

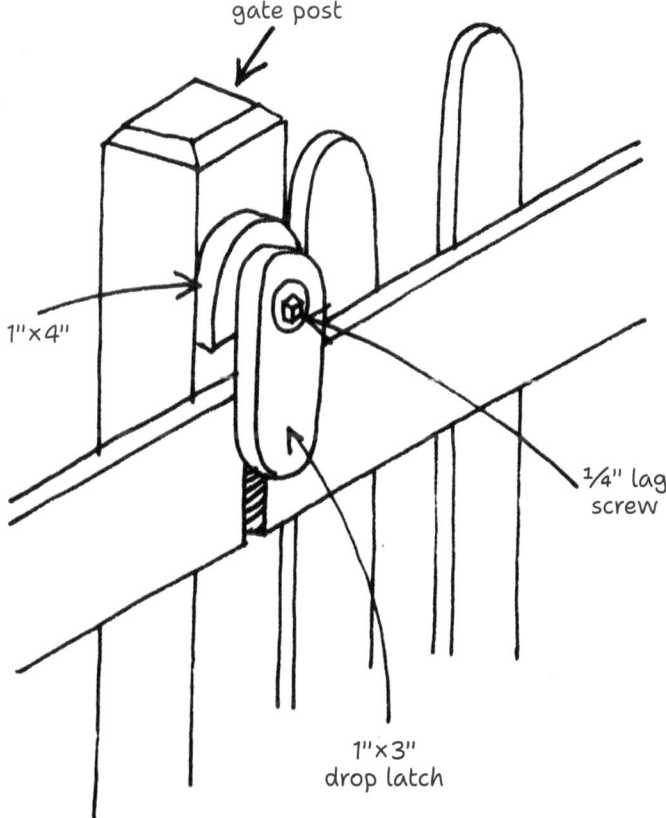

gate post

1"×4"

¼" lag
screw

1"×3"
drop latch

A drop latch swivels to hold the
top board of the gate in place.

# STILES

A stile is a wonderful invention to reduce the wear and tear you will put on a fence if you crawl over, under, or through it with any regularity.

Use a stile only where the crossings are occasional. Using one to cross a fence between garden and compost pile would become a tiring nuisance. But one across a fence on a favorite walk through meadows can be a delight and a place to rest and meditate for a moment. Children love them. They can be houses, castles, or ships. A little-used one on a garden fence is ideal for potted plants—but only a few plants or you will trip the passers-up-and-over.

Some people walking over a stile that puts them at fence-top height may find the altitude disconcerting. If so, mount a sturdy post beside the stile that reaches up to at least 4 feet above it to provide security and an assist in balancing.

Here is a variety of models, all of them comparatively easy to build.

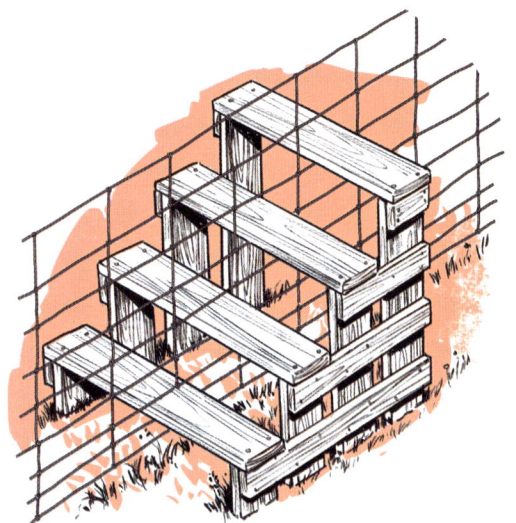

stair stile

triangular stile

**ladder stile**

**leaning ladder stile**

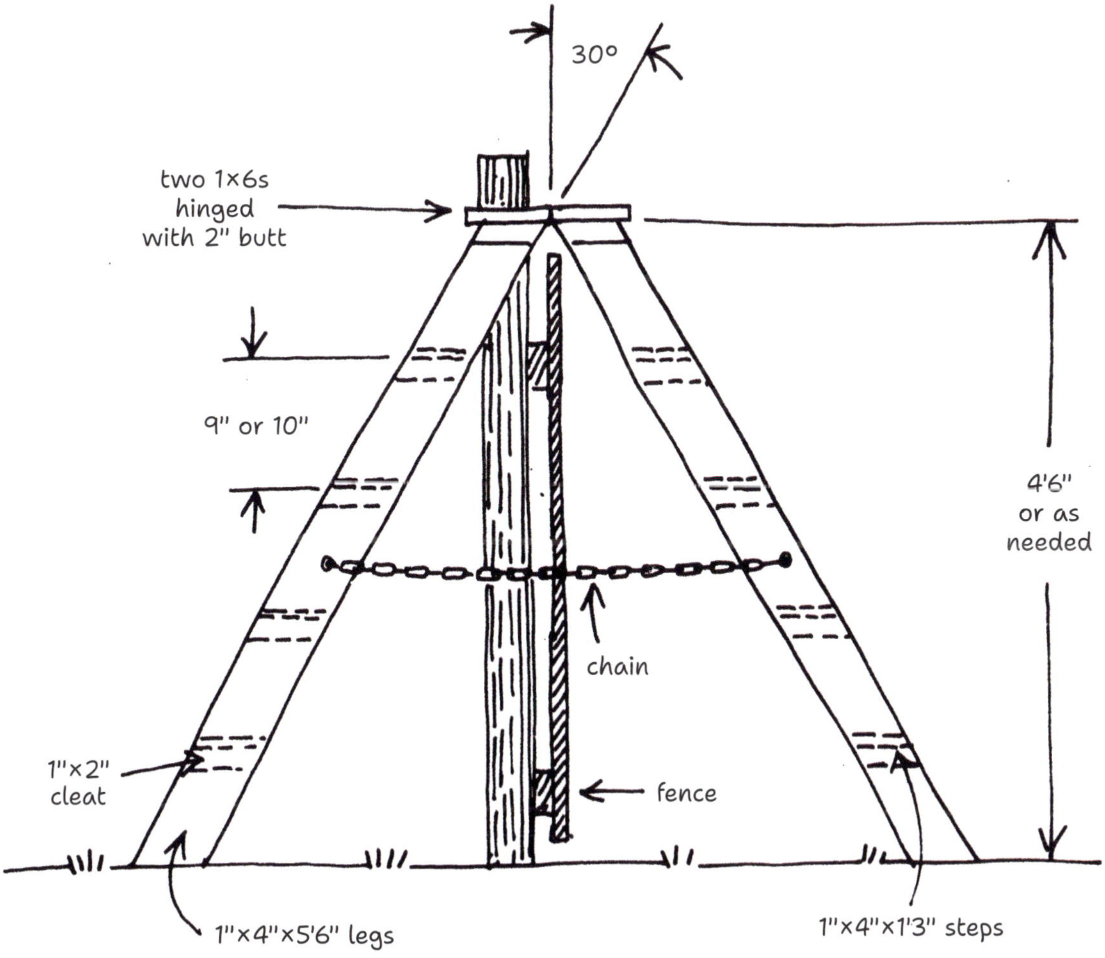

30°

two 1×6s
hinged
with 2" butt

9" or 10"

4'6"
or as
needed

chain

1"×2"
cleat

fence

1"×4"×5'6" legs

1"×4"×1'3" steps

Grapevine Supports, page 116

Bird Feeders, page 122

Birdhouse, page 118

Picnic Bench, page 84

Massive Pot, page 94

Garden Bench, page 79

# GRAPEVINE SUPPORTS

For a satisfying venture, try growing grapes. There are varieties for nearly every section of the country.

Grapes demand a minimum of care, and most of that is at a time that doesn't interfere with other gardening tasks. They are remarkably free of disease. Best of all is the harvest of grapes, eaten fresh, used in jellies or jams, or squeezed for the juice and the wine that may follow.

If your home or garage is built so there is a south-facing wall that can be used, you can grow grapes against that. Support for a grapevine built against a building should be:

- **Sturdy.** It will have a lot of weight on it when the vines stretch across and are heavy with grapes.

- **Accessible.** Build near enough to the ground so that the grapes can be picked.

- **Away from the roof.** If built under the slope of a roof, leave space between the vines and the roof for runoff of rain and, in cooler climates, the sliding of melting snow.

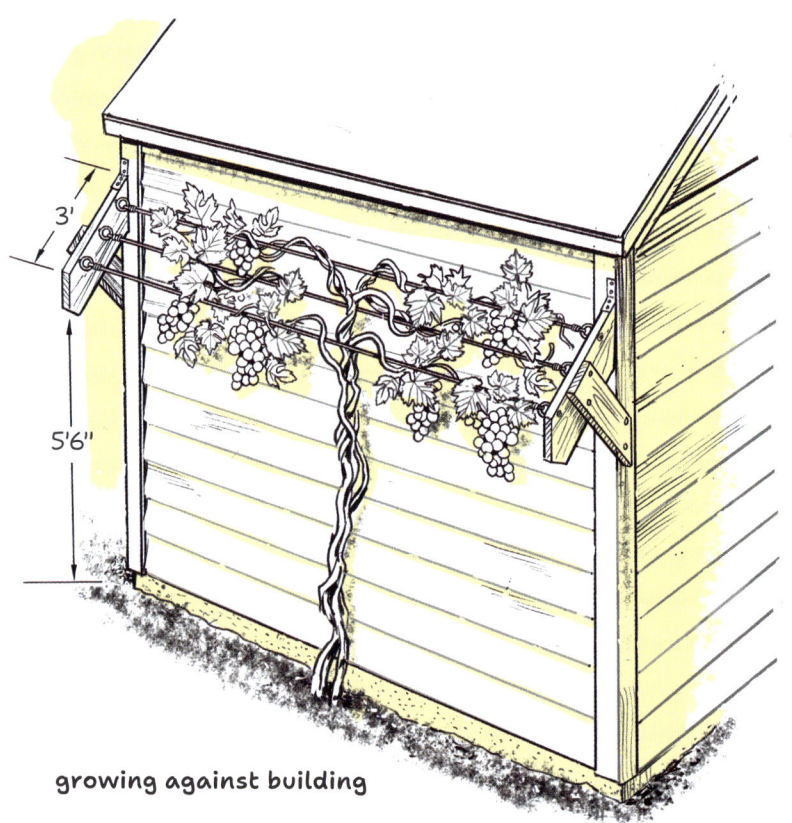

3'

5'6"

growing against building

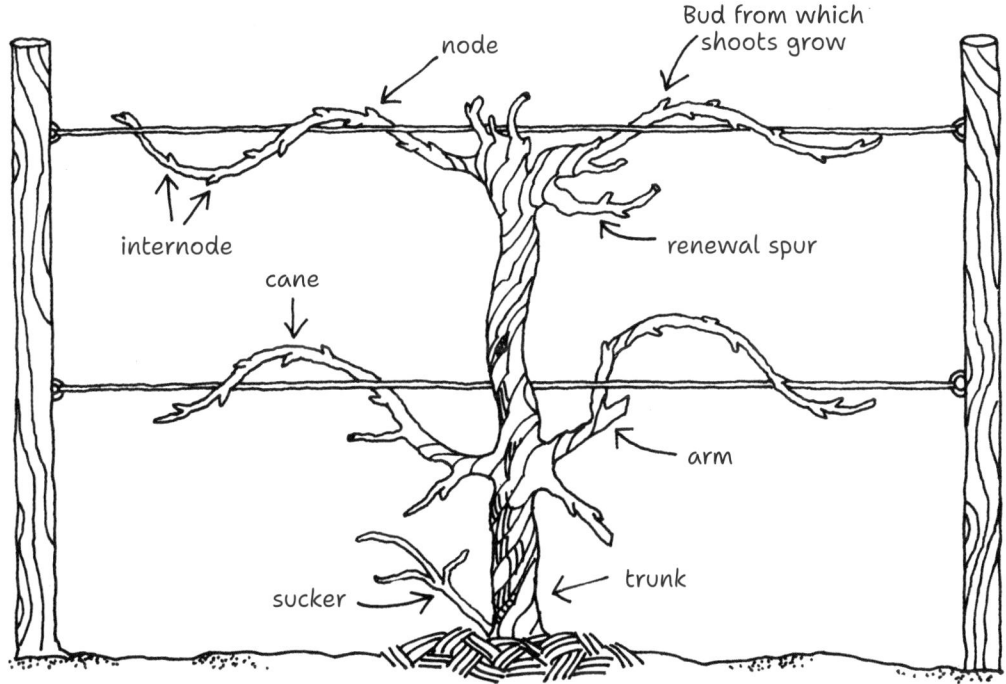

**Kniffin system**

Attach two 3-foot pieces of lumber to the garage at an angle, roughly 5½ feet above the ground. Connect them with three strands of wire to support the grapevines.

Read any book about growing grapes and you will probably see the Kniffin system explained. This system has two wires between poles, one wire above the other. The two wires hold the vine, pruned to four arms. You need not be tied down to such a system for your two or three vines.

The first year of planting, the vine will need only a post so it will be encouraged to grow upwards. The second year the vine will need a trellis. A simple way is to plant the vines 8 feet apart, with stout poles set 2½ feet into the ground, midway between the plants and, on the ends of the row, 4 feet beyond the end plants. If the posts are 8 feet long, one strand of wire (9-gauge galvanized is good) can stretch across the tops of the posts, and the second wire can be tied 2 feet below the top.

The weight of the vines puts an inward pull on those poles, particularly the end ones. They can be anchored with deadmen or braced with a post, reaching from the top of each end post diagonally to the ground near the vine.

Grapes want sunshine, good air circulation (put rows 8 feet apart), and rich soil. Provide these and you and your grandchildren will enjoy your vines.

# BIRDHOUSES

Give your neighborhood birds a home and they will give you a hand with the insect problems in your garden. Plus, they're just fun to watch.

If you want birds around your home and garden, however, birdhouses alone aren't enough. Plant some trees, shrubs, or vines that offer them food, and they'll come a-flying.

Here are some suggestions for building birdhouses:

- **Build for the bird's pleasure, not for your own.** Don't paint the birdhouse with brilliant colors that may attract predators, and paint it at least a few weeks before the birds will occupy it so the smell of paint will be gone.

- **Pick a site carefully.** It should be safe from cats, face away from the prevailing wind, and not tilt upward, which would invite rain inside.

- **Space them out.** Don't place several houses for the same kind of birds closely together. Birds have a strong territorial instinct, and several houses close together will only promote ill feelings among neighbors.

- **Keep cleaning in mind.** Build the house so its interior can be easily cleaned. This means hinging one side or the bottom so that it will swing open. Clean the house as soon as the birds desert it, and another couple may occupy it that summer.

- **Plan for drainage.** Drill small holes in the bottom for drainage.

- **Use the proper dimensions** and bore the correct-size holes (see table on page 121) for entrance. Too large an entrance makes small birds vulnerable to attack or displacement by larger birds.

# Easy Birdhouse

This easy birdhouse is built of one 40½-inch piece of 1×6 and one more piece that is 8″ × 8½″ for the roof. Cut as shown, nail together, provide a couple weather-resistant hinges for the roof (for cleaning) and don't forget the drainage holes in the bottom. Hang it 10 feet above ground in the spring and watch the birds move in.

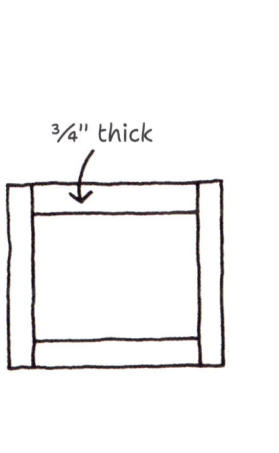

¾″ thick

**bottom**

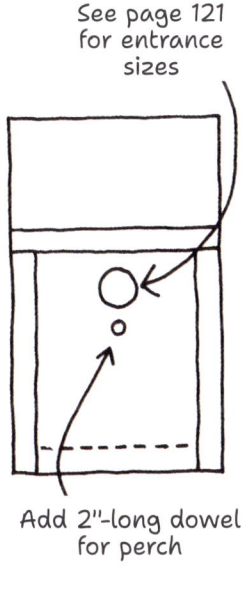

See page 121 for entrance sizes

Add 2″-long dowel for perch

**front**

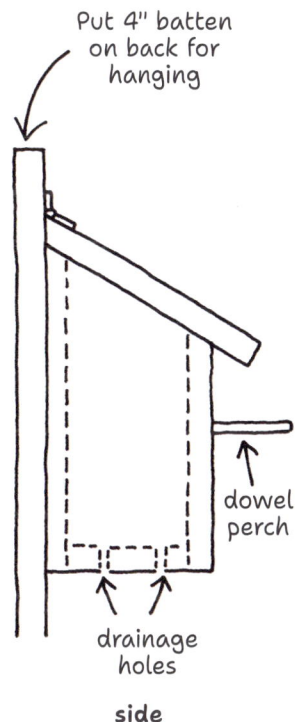

Put 4″ batten on back for hanging

dowel perch

drainage holes

**side**

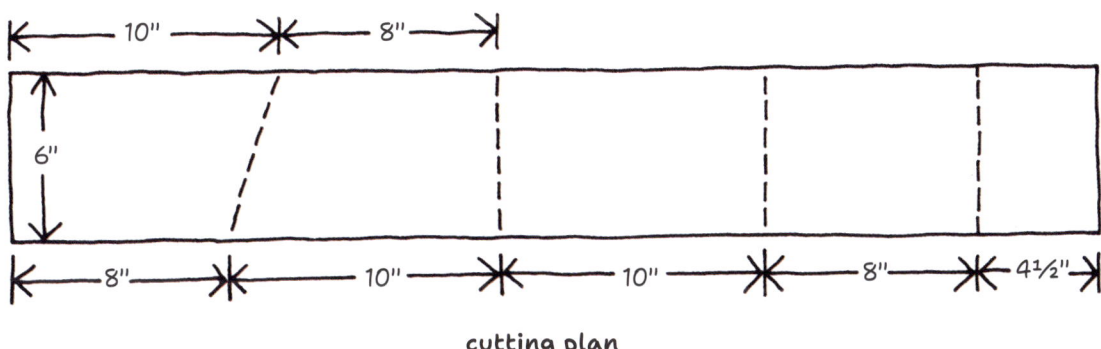

10″

8″

6″

8″ 10″ 10″ 8″ 4½″

**cutting plan**

# Robin's Shelf

Robins do not like the confinement of a birdhouse. And they are particularly careless about their choice of a nest location. They will build where there is much human traffic, then complain loudly about that traffic keeping their young nervous and awake. Help them solve their problems with a shelf that provides a roof over their heads, sides for partial protection, and an 8-inch square base for the nest.

## Nesting Shelves for Birds

(one or more sides open)

| Kind of Bird | Min. Floor Size | Depth of Box | Preferred Height above Ground |
|---|---|---|---|
| Robin | 6" × 8" | 8" | 6–15' |
| Barn Swallow | 6" × 6" | 6" | 8–12' |
| Song Sparrow | 6" × 6" | 6" | 1–3' |
| Phoebe | 6" × 6" | 6" | 8–12' |

## Birdhouse Dimensions

| Kind of Bird | Floor Size | Box Depth | Height of Entrance above Floor | Diameter of Entrance | Height above Ground |
|---|---|---|---|---|---|
| Bluebird | 5" × 5" | 8" | 6" | 1½" | 5–10' |
| Chickadee | 4" × 4" | 8–10" | 6–8" | 1⅛" | 6–15' |
| Duck, Wood | 10" × 18" | 10–24" | 12–16" | 4" | 10–20' |
| Flycatcher, Crested | 6" × 6" | 8–10" | 6–8" | 2" | 8–20' |
| Finch, House | 6" × 6" | 6" | 4" | 2" | 8–12' |
| Flicker | 7" × 7" | 16–18" | 14–16" | 2½" | 6–20' |
| Kestrel, American | 8" × 8" | 12–15" | 9–12" | 3" | 10–30' |
| Nuthatch | 4" × 4" | 8–10" | 6–8" | 1¼" | 12–20' |
| Owl, Barn | 10" × 18" | 15–18" | 4" | 6" | 12–18' |
| Owl, Saw-Whet | 6" × 6" | 10–12" | 8–10" | 2½" | 12–20' |
| Owl, Screech | 8" × 8" | 12–15" | 9–12" | 3" | 10–30' |
| Purple Martin | 6" × 6" | 6" | 1" | 2½" | 15–20' |
| Starling | 6" × 6" | 16–18" | 14–16" | 2" | 10–25' |
| Swallows, Violet-Green and Tree | 5" × 5" | 6" | 1–5" | 1½" | 10–15' |
| Titmouse | 4" × 4" | 8–10" | 6–8" | 1¼" | 6–15' |
| Woodpecker, Downy | 4" × 4" | 8–10" | 6–8" | 1¼" | 6–20' |
| Woodpeckers, Golden Fronted and Redheaded | 6" × 6" | 12–15" | 9–12" | 2" | 12–20' |
| Woodpecker, Hairy | 6" × 6" | 12–15" | 9–12" | 1½" | 12–20' |
| Wren, Carolina | 4" × 4" | 6–8" | 4–6" | 1¼" | 6–10' |
| Wrens, House and Bewick's | 4" × 4" | 6–8" | 4–6" | 1–1¼" | 6–10' |

# BIRD FEEDERS

Bird feeders can help birds survive harsh winters, and they're a lovely way to attract more birds to your yard.

Here are only a few of the many bird feeders that can be built quickly and inexpensively. If they're kept well filled with birdseed during the winter, you will never lack for lively, chattering companionship.

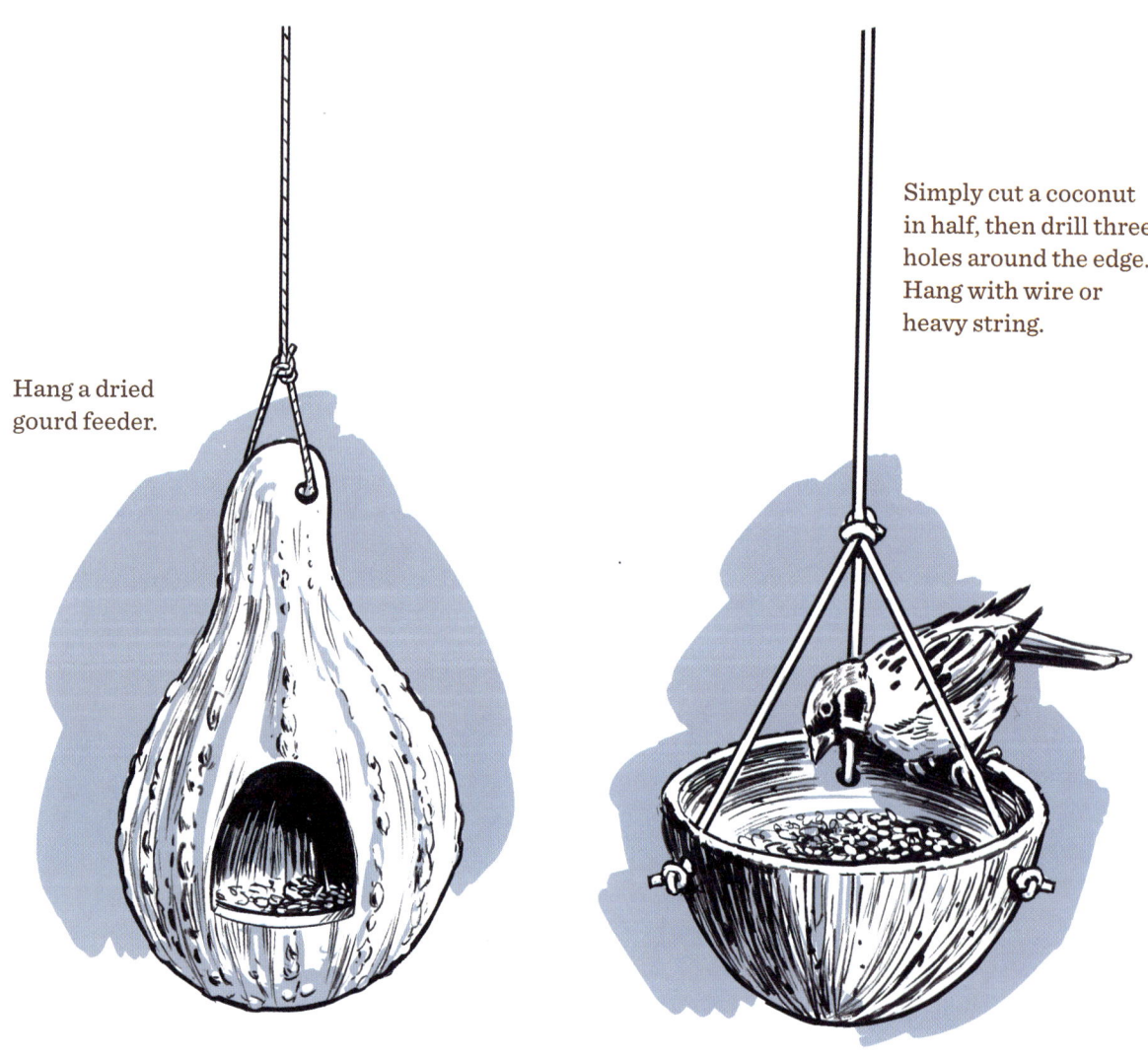

Simply cut a coconut in half, then drill three holes around the edge. Hang with wire or heavy string.

Hang a dried gourd feeder.

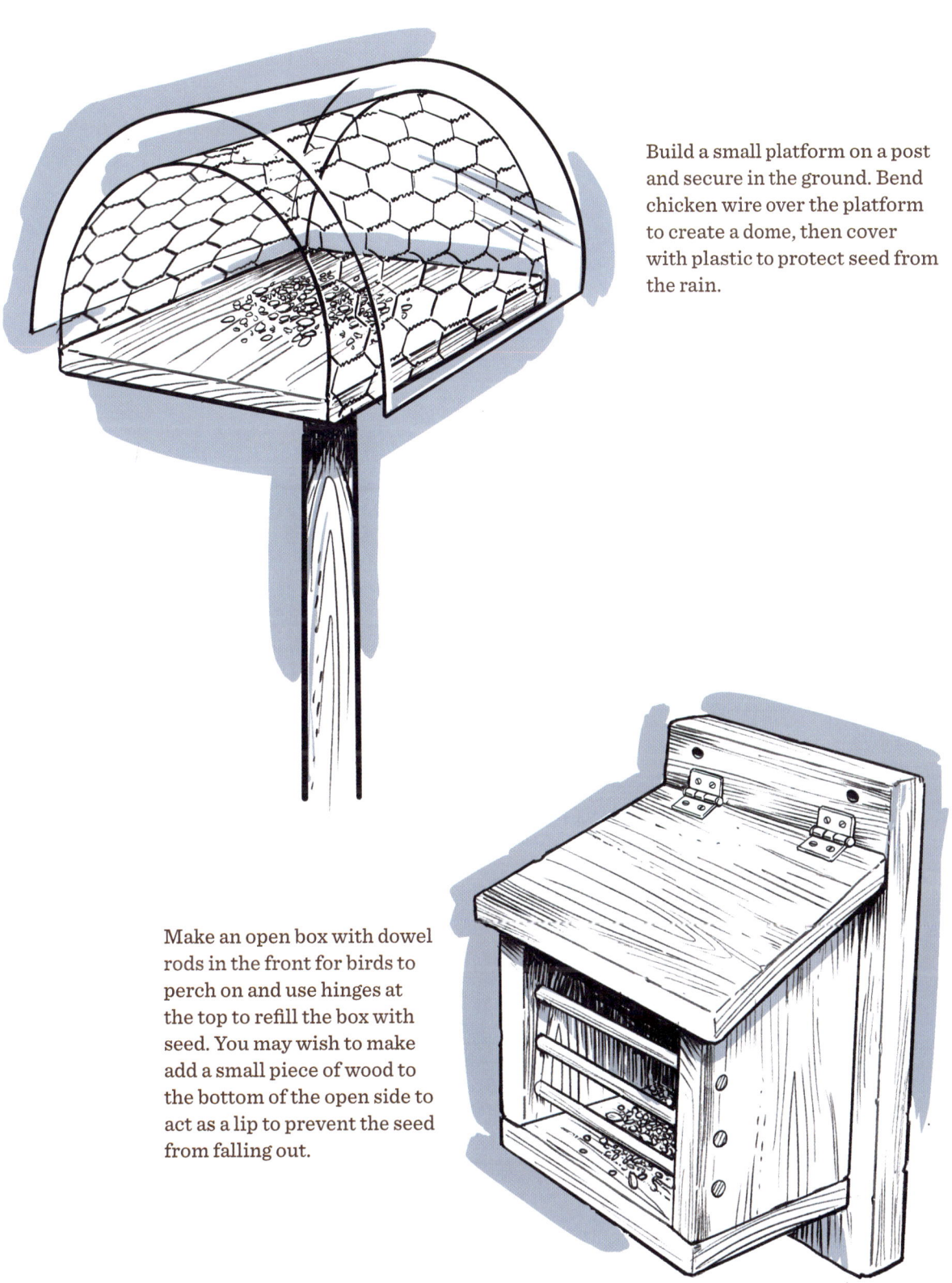

Build a small platform on a post and secure in the ground. Bend chicken wire over the platform to create a dome, then cover with plastic to protect seed from the rain.

Make an open box with dowel rods in the front for birds to perch on and use hinges at the top to refill the box with seed. You may wish to make add a small piece of wood to the bottom of the open side to act as a lip to prevent the seed from falling out.

# POULTRY HOUSE

This is an ideal house for a small flock—and for the person who prefers floor housing instead of the cage systems used today by most commercial egg producers.

It will provide clean, dry housing throughout the year, can be ventilated, and should be insulated in northern climates. For the person raising the chickens, it has a small storage room.

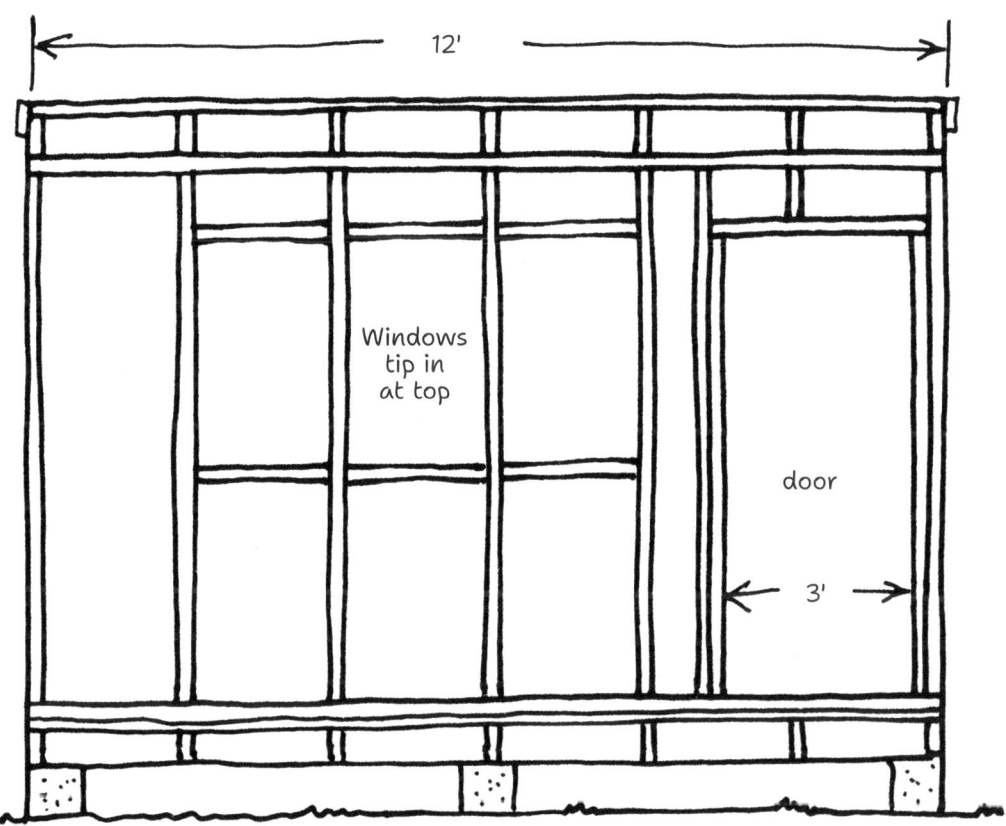

12'

Windows
tip in
at top

door

3'

front

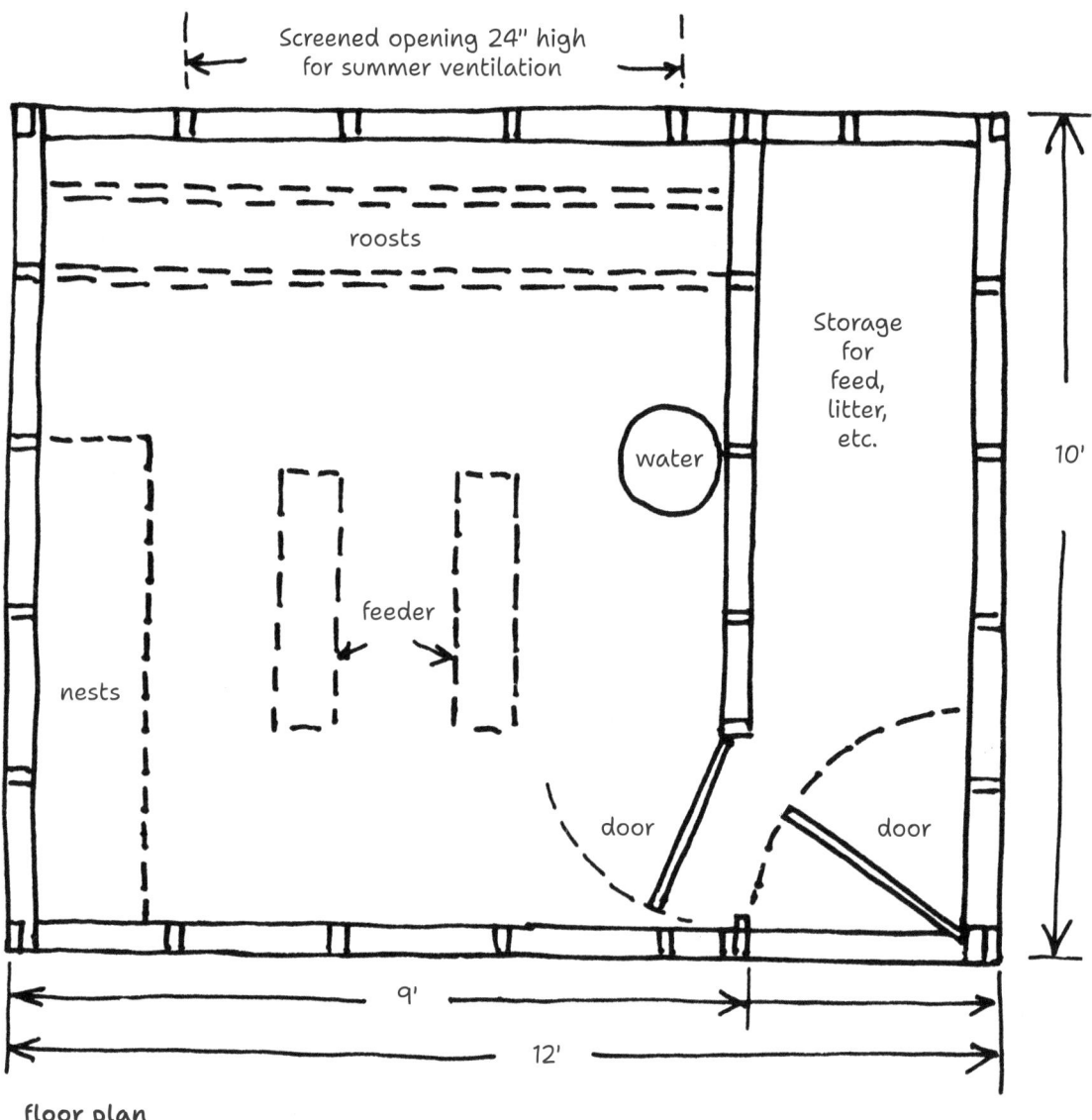

Screened opening 24" high
for summer ventilation

roosts

Storage
for
feed,
litter,
etc.

water

10'

nests

feeder

door

door

9'

12'

**floor plan**

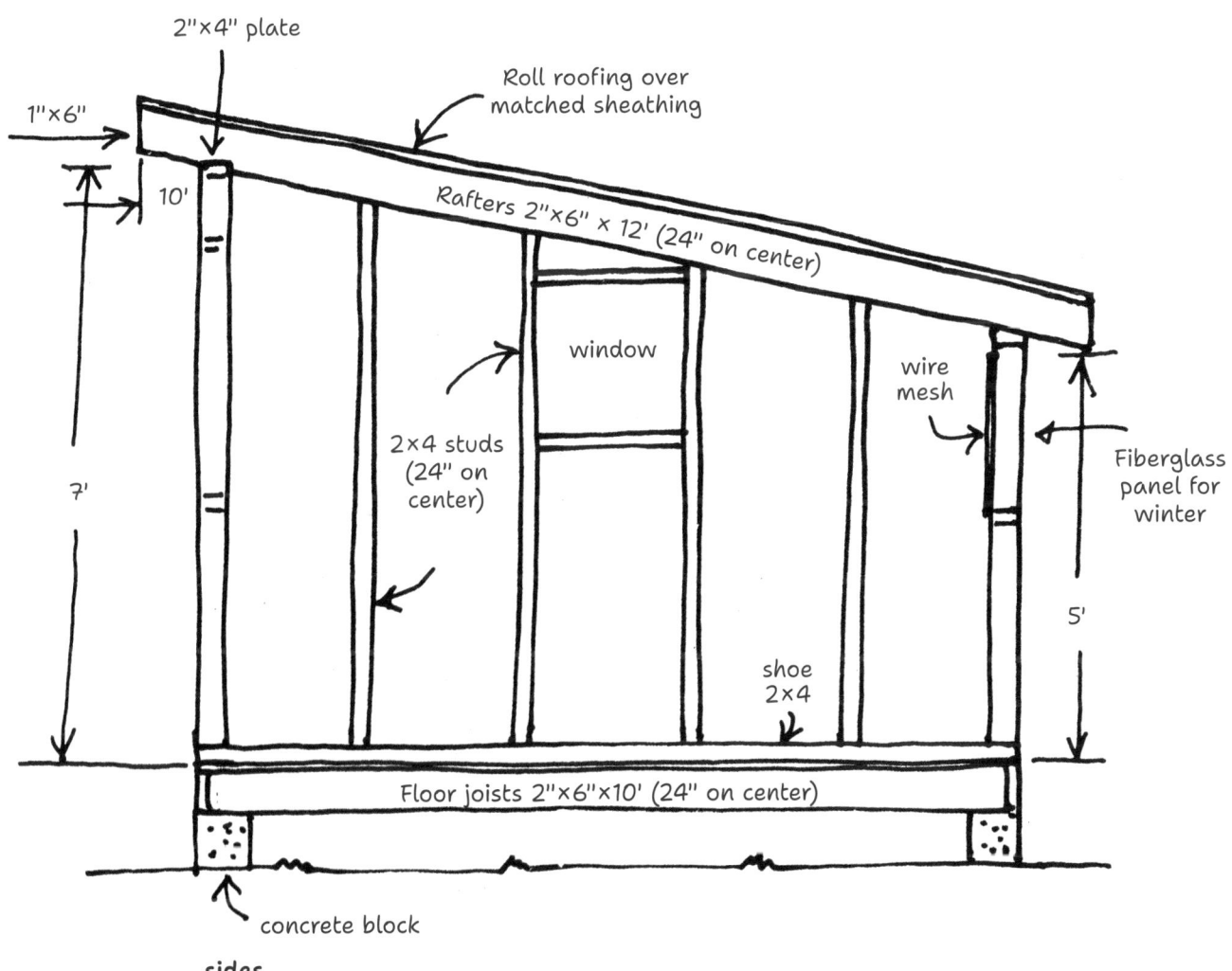

2"×4" plate

Roll roofing over matched sheathing

1"×6"

10'

Rafters 2"×6" × 12' (24" on center)

window

2×4 studs (24" on center)

wire mesh

Fiberglass panel for winter

7'

5'

shoe 2×4

Floor joists 2"×6"×10' (24" on center)

concrete block

**sides**

# CHICKEN FEEDERS

Chicken feeders should be large enough to supply the flock's needs for a day or more without wasting feed.

The design of the feeder is closely tied to the control of waste. Devices to prevent waste include an anti-roost spring on top of the feeder and a lip on the side of the hopper to prevent birds from beaking out feed. If the feeder is never more than half-filled, much feed will be saved.

Here are three feeders you can build.

## Roofed Feeder

This 5-foot-long feeder has a roof to prevent any roosting birds from casting droppings inside of it and to keep out the elements. It's made from one 8-foot 1×12, one 12-foot 1×10, one 10-foot 1×4, one 16-foot 1×2, and one 10-foot ¼″ × 1¼″.

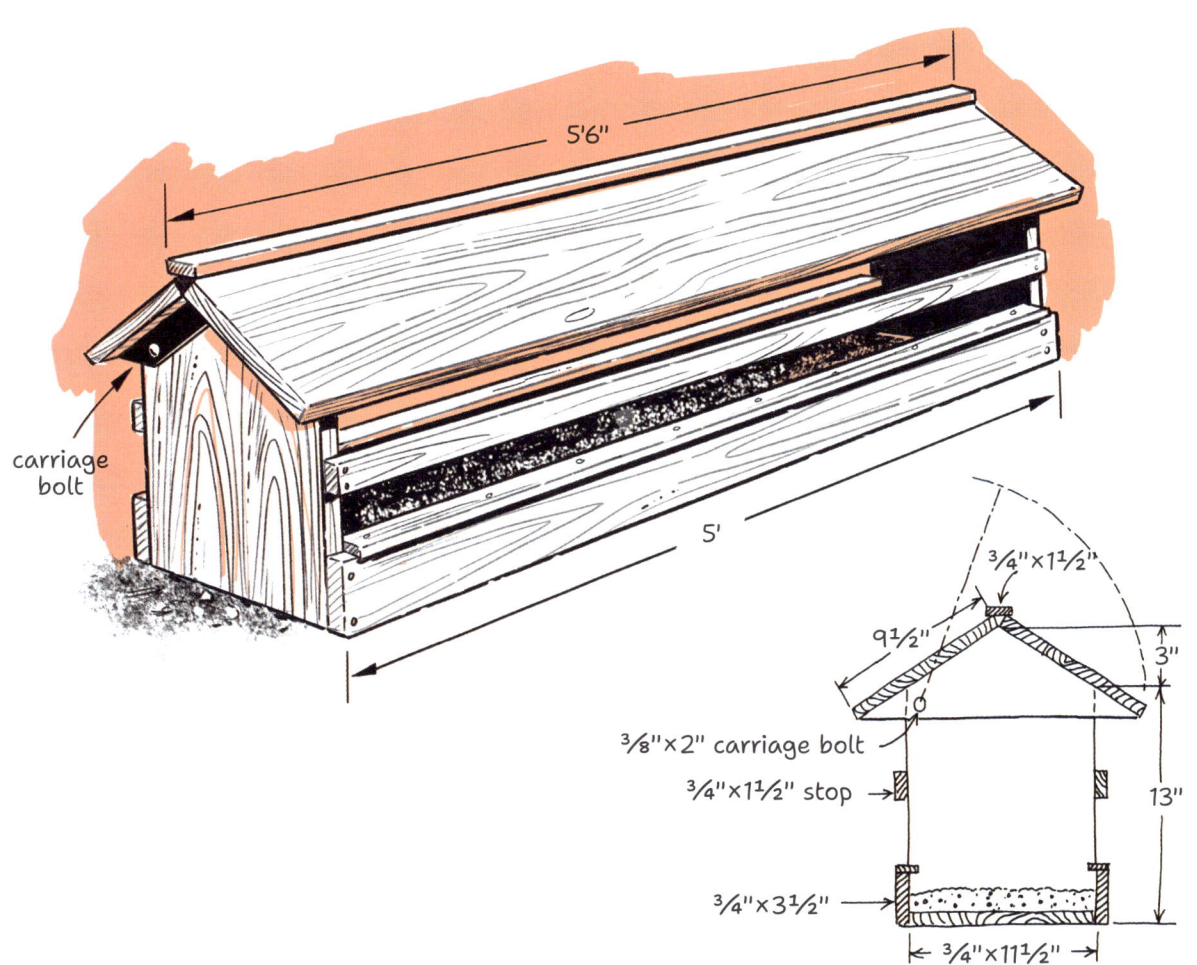

carriage bolt

5'6"

5'

¾″×1½″

9½″

3"

⅜″×2" carriage bolt

¾″×1½″ stop

13"

¾″×3½″

¾″×11½″

# Adjustable Feeder

This feeder can be raised and lowered as needed by twisting the wing nuts, and a lip on the side prevents birds from beaking out feed. It's made using one 8-foot 1×8, one 12-foot 1×4, and one 6-foot ¼″ × 1¼″ .

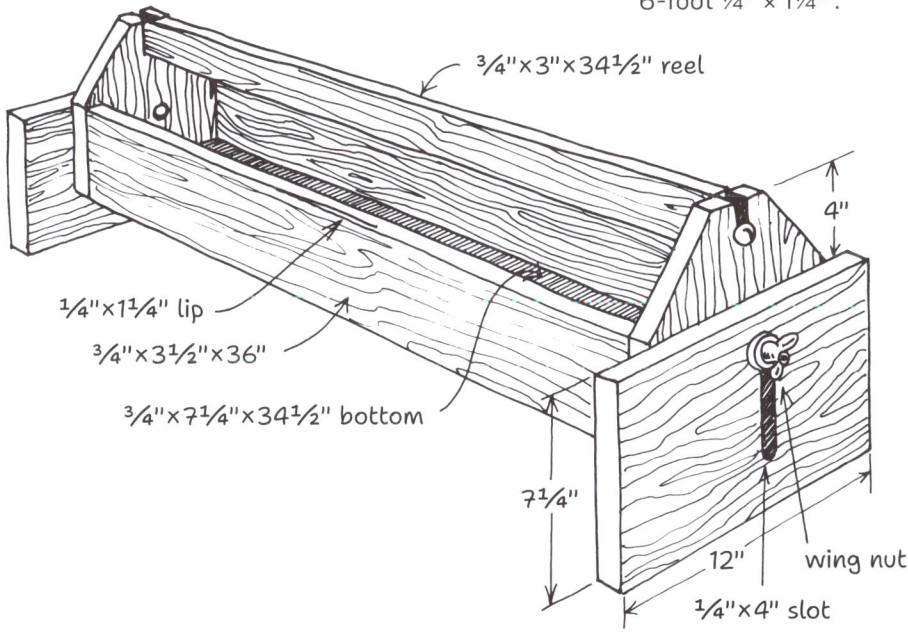

¾"×3"×34½" reel

4"

¼"×1¼" lip

¾"×3½"×36"

¾"×7¼"×34½" bottom

7¼"

12"

¼"×4" slot

wing nut

# Anti-Roost Feeder

A wire spring on the top of this feeder prevents birds from roosting on top. It's made from one 12-foot 1×6 and one 6-foot ¼″ × 1¼″.

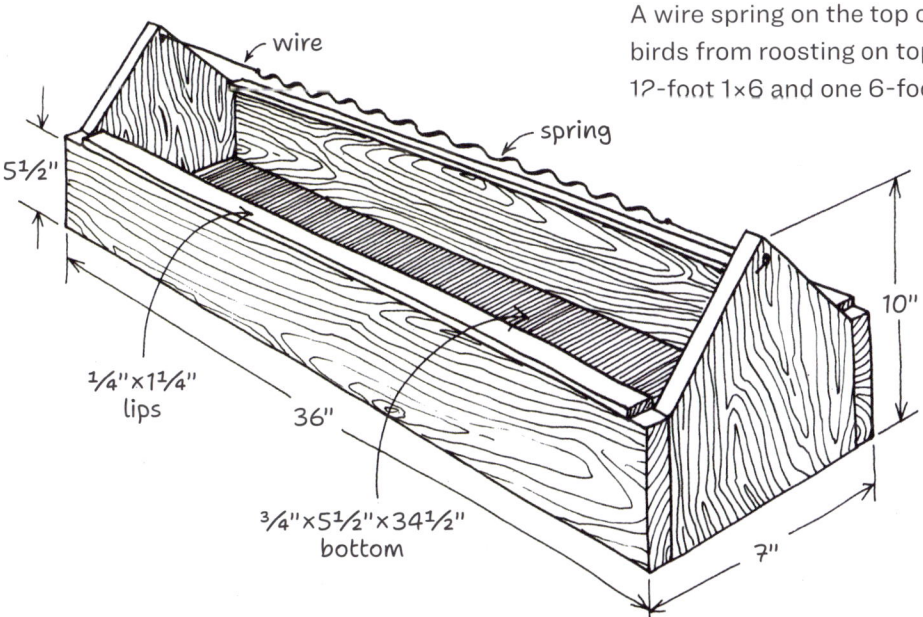

wire

spring

5½"

¼"×1¼" lips

36"

¾"×5½"×34½" bottom

10"

7"

# CHICKEN WATERERS

Hens and chickens must have access to clean, fresh water at all times. For every pound of feed consumed, laying birds will drink about a quart of water, and they will drink much more than that in hot weather.

A waterer made from a gallon can and a pan works very well for a small flock. Simply make holes on either side of the can as shown, add water, place a metal pan that is larger in diameter than the can on top, then turn the can and pan upside down. The water will empty out through the holes and into the pan.

If you have running water piped into the house, you will probably buy an automatic water fountain and eliminate one task from your list of daily chores. If you do, place it on a platform you can build out of five pieces of 1" × 4" × 30", nailed into a square with a center brace as shown and covered with 1×2 welded wire mesh, nailed in place with galvanized fence staples. This platform will provide drier conditions around the fountain and lessen the amount of litter material that finds its way into the drinking reservoir.

Make two holes on
either side of can

On either side of a gallon can,
add holes about ¾ inch from the
top. Add water to the can, then
place a metal pan on top. Turn
upside down.

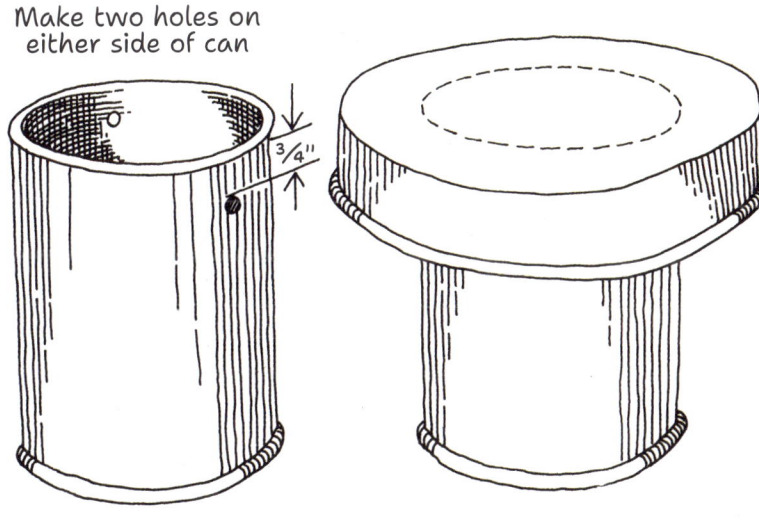

¾"

watering can

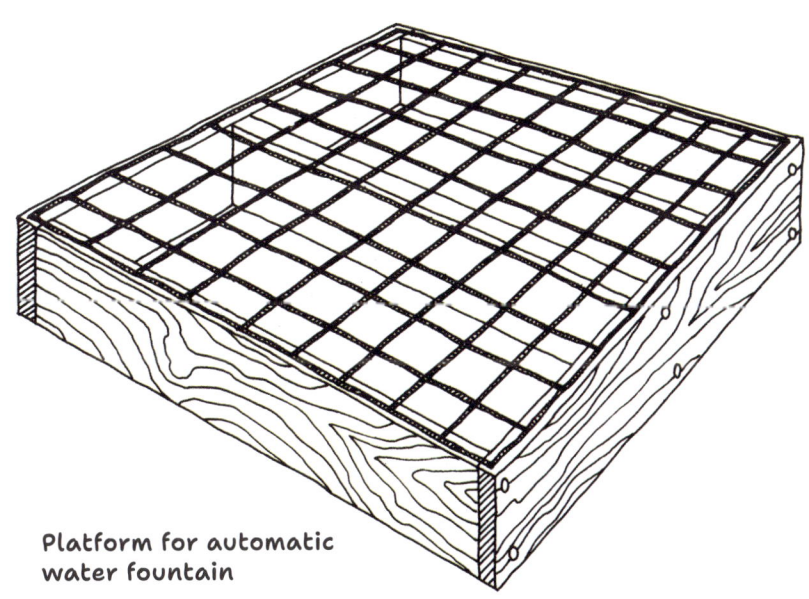

Platform for automatic
water fountain

Poultry House, page 124

# NESTS

Nests provide chickens with a place to lay eggs and can simplify the chore of collecting them.

You'll need one individual nest, or 1 square foot of community nest, for every four laying birds in your flock. Individual nests should be at least 1 foot long, wide, and high. For community nests, provide two 9 × 12-inch openings for each 20 square feet of nest space. Provide a landing board in front of all openings and place nests about 2 feet above the floor.

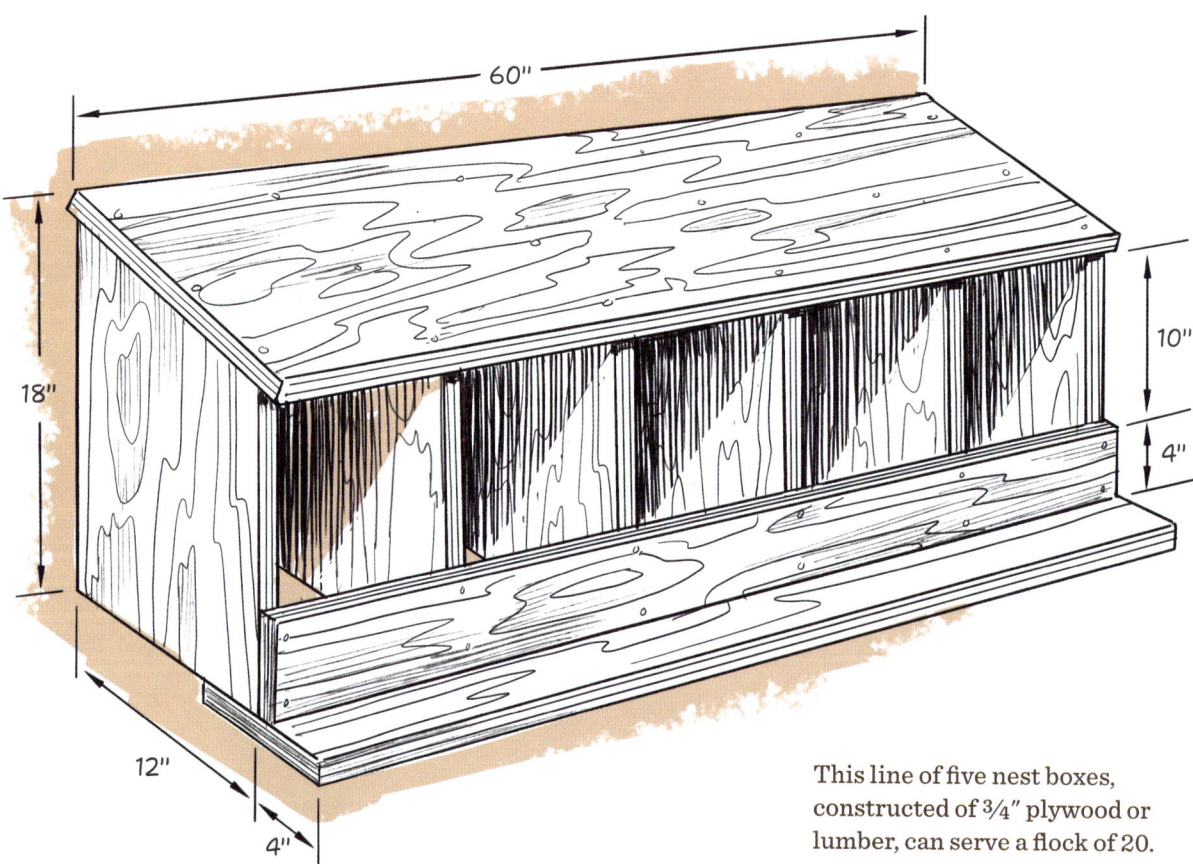

This line of five nest boxes, constructed of ¾" plywood or lumber, can serve a flock of 20.

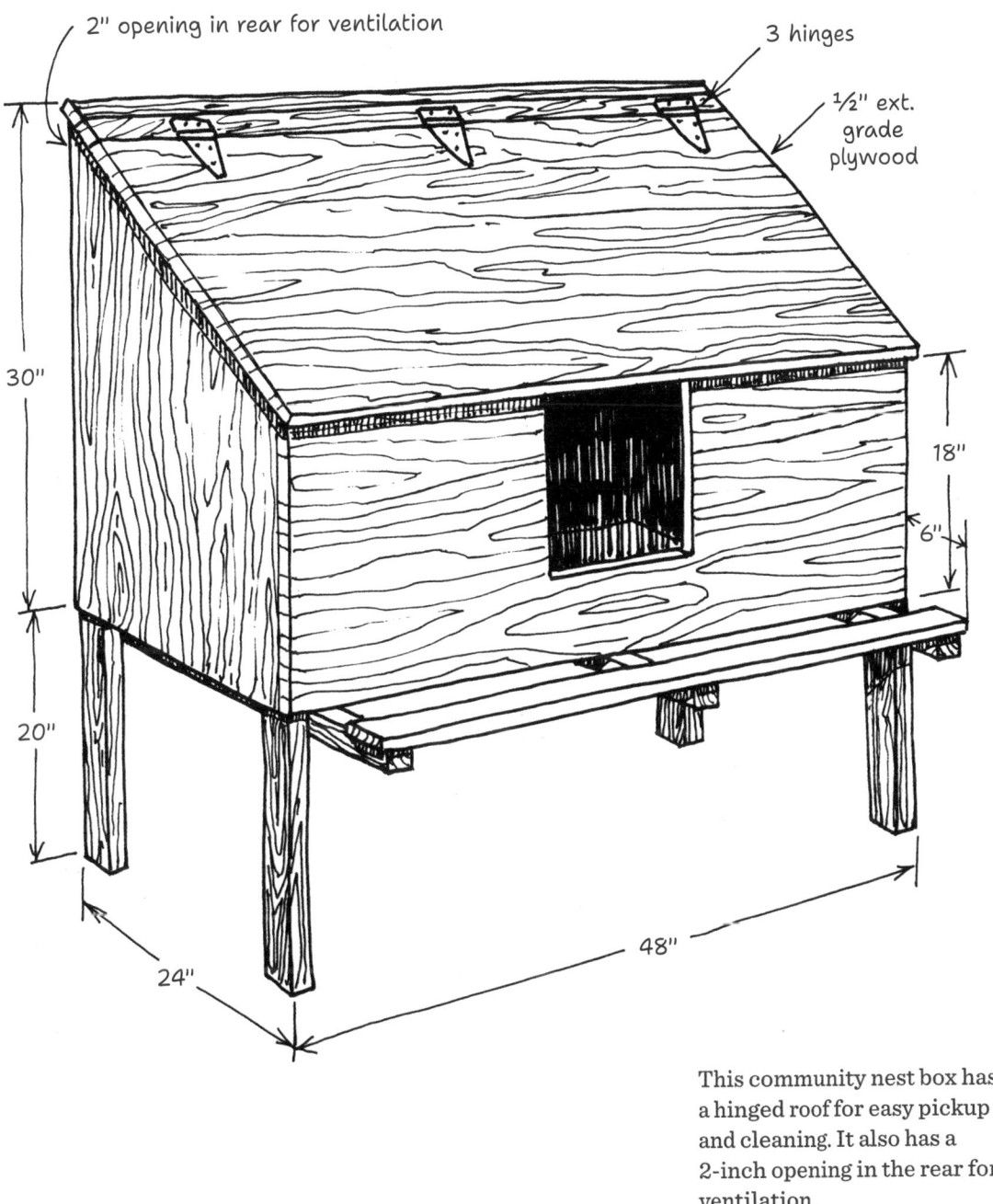

2" opening in rear for ventilation

3 hinges

½" ext. grade plywood

30"

18"

6"

20"

24"

48"

This community nest box has a hinged roof for easy pickup and cleaning. It also has a 2-inch opening in the rear for ventilation.

# EGG CANDLING LIGHT

If you have a rooster, you'll need some way to determine if your eggs are fertile. If many eggs need to be checked, a candling light such as this will speed the task.

Eggs are candled to determine whether they are fertile. The infertile egg will appear clear before the light. If the egg is fertile, you will see a small spot (the embryo) and a web of blood vessels.

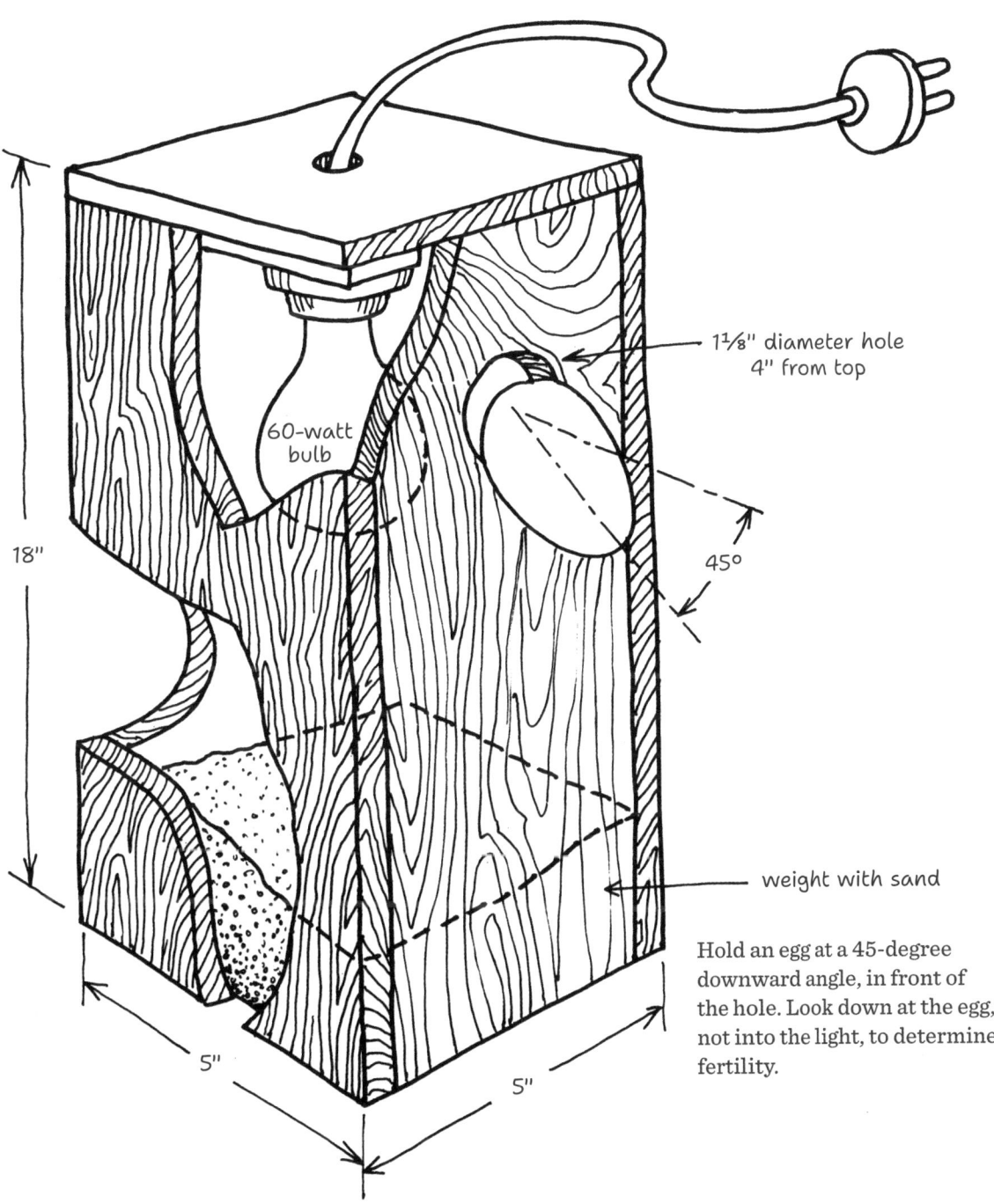

1⅛" diameter hole
4" from top

60-watt
bulb

45°

18"

weight with sand

Hold an egg at a 45-degree
downward angle, in front of
the hole. Look down at the egg,
not into the light, to determine
fertility.

5"

5"

# INCUBATOR

You can incubate chicken eggs at home with some careful planning and attention to detail. The thrill of watching the first chick peck through the shell is often worth the extra effort.

A good setting hen provides ideal incubating conditions for 9 or 10 eggs. Duplicating these conditions requires some careful work, since temperature, ventilation, and humidity are important.

The temperature must be between 100°F and 103°F (37.8°C to 39.4°C) and should be held at 102°F (38.9°C). The humidity level during the initial period of the 21 days of incubation varies from 83°F to 88°F (28.3°C to 31.1°C) (wet bulb thermometer) depending on the type of eggs. Increase the humidity to 90°F to 95°F (32.2°C to 35°C) (wet bulb) in the last three or four days before hatching.

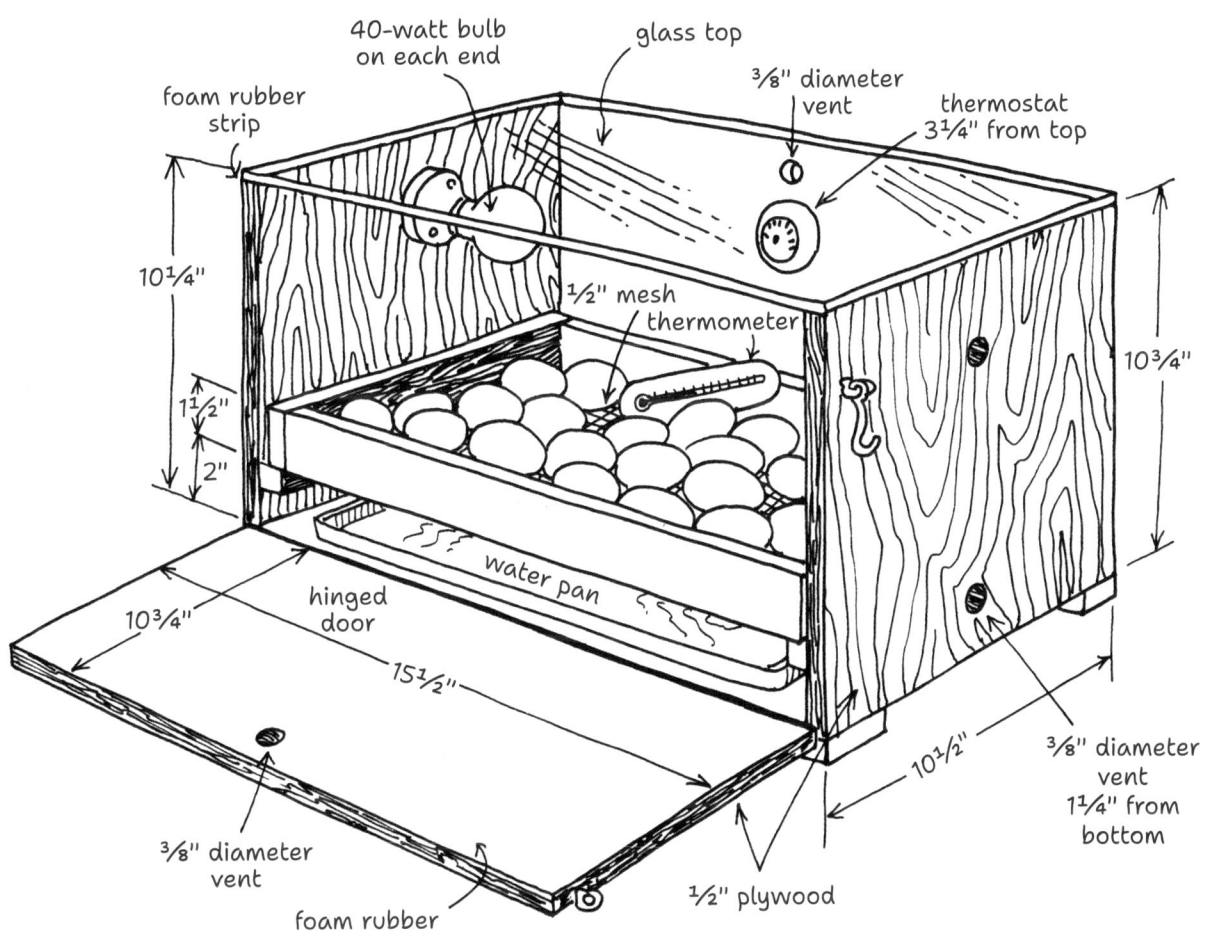

40-watt bulb on each end

glass top

³⁄₈" diameter vent

thermostat 3¼" from top

foam rubber strip

10¼"

1½"

2"

½" mesh thermometer

water pan

hinged door

10¾"

15½"

10½"

10¾"

³⁄₈" diameter vent 1¼" from bottom

³⁄₈" diameter vent

foam rubber

½" plywood

If the exacting work of incubation is within your capabilities, try building this incubator. Traditionally the heat source would be an incandescent or halogen bulb, but a ceramic heat emitter (which screws into the same socket as a lightbulb) is a good alternative.

# Enhance Your Outdoor Spaces with More Books from Storey

### *The Backyard Homestead Book of Building Projects*
by Spike Carlsen

Improve your garden, farm, or yard with these 76 simple DIY projects. From plant supports and clotheslines to a chicken coop, a root cellar, and even a complete greenhouse, most of the projects are suitable for complete beginners, and all use only basic tools and easy-to-find materials.

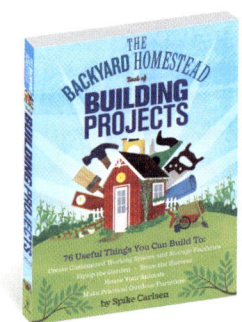

### *Fences for Home and Garden*
by Jeff Beneke

Learn how to choose and build the right fence to meet your needs. This comprehensive guide includes step-by-step illustrated instructions for building wood, masonry, metal, and living fences that will last for years.

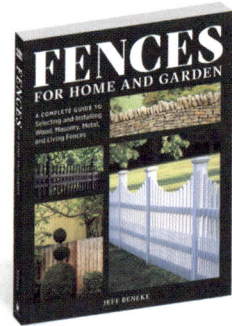

### *Tree Houses within Reach*
by Derek "Deek" Diedricksen

Ever dreamed of building your own tree house? This lively showcase of 30 wildly different and eclectic tree houses, ranging from simple platform structures to raised tiny houses, office spaces, and play houses, will inspire and delight you.